Supporting Early Learning through Rhymes and Stories

T0384855

This book shows how adults can bring rhymes and stories to life with young children and support children's early steps in communication and literacy. Focusing on the use of rhyme, rhythm and repetition in nursery rhymes and traditional tales from around the world, it provides a wealth of practical ideas for using rhymes and stories one-on-one, in small groups or with whole classes.

Drawing from the culmination of their many years of combined experience, the two authors link the theoretical understanding of language and communication with the practical use of rhymes and oral storytelling in the classroom, in the nursery and at home. Early chapters (or Part I) provide a rationale for using rhyme, rhythm and repetition to inspire children to play with words and develop a love of language, building a foundation for literacy learning. Part II consists of ten lively chapters featuring original and re-imagined traditional fairy tales, containing:

- Accompanying rhymes to use with children
- Key themes including friendship, kindness, compassion and generosity
- Follow-up activities for extending children's vocabulary, building their confidence and developing critical thinking
- Suggestions of using voices, facial expressions, gestures, props and puppets to enrich children's emotional, imaginative and intellectual experience

This delightful and practical book will be valuable reading for all adults wanting to support young children's creative learning through enjoyable and valuable experiences.

Sarah Cousins (EdD) is an experienced early years teacher, leader, consultant and lecturer. She held various leadership roles at universities, including the University of Warwick. Sarah has published on love in early years, emotional and social learning in early years, mathematics anxiety and adult learning in Higher Education.

Hilary Minns (PhD) was an early years teacher and headteacher of a primary school in the Midlands before becoming a lecturer at the University of Warwick. Her publications include works on young children's emergent literacy learning in a variety of historical, social and cultural settings.

Supporting Early Learning through Rhymes and Stories

Sarah Cousins and Hilary Minns

Routledge
Taylor & Francis Group

LONDON AND NEW YORK

Designed cover image: © Getty Images

First published 2024
by Routledge
4 Park Square, Milton Park, Abingdon, Oxon, OX14 4RN

and by Routledge
605 Third Avenue, New York, NY 10158

Routledge is an imprint of the Taylor & Francis Group, an informa business

© 2024 Sarah Cousins and Hilary Minns

British Library Cataloguing-in-Publication Data
A catalogue record for this book is available from the British Library

Library of Congress Cataloging-in-Publication Data
Names: Cousins, Sarah B., author. | Minns, Hilary, author.
Title: Supporting early learning through rhymes and stories / Sarah Cousins and Hilary Minns.
Description: First edition. | Abingdon, Oxon ; New York, NY : Routledge, 2024. | Includes bibliographical references. |
Identifiers: LCCN 2023027286 (print) | LCCN 2023027287 (ebook) | ISBN 9781032415468 (hardback) | ISBN 9781032415451 (paperback) | ISBN 9781003358633 (ebook)
Subjects: LCSH: Storytelling in education. | Stories in rhyme--Study and teaching (Early childhood) | Nursery rhymes--Study and teaching (Early childhood)
Classification: LCC LB1042 .C498 2024 (print) | LCC LB1042 (ebook) | DDC 372.67/7044--dc23/eng/20230912
LC record available at https://lccn.loc.gov/2023027286
LC ebook record available at https://lccn.loc.gov/2023027287

ISBN: 978-1-032-41546-8 (hbk)
ISBN: 978-1-032-41545-1 (pbk)
ISBN: 978-1-003-35863-3 (ebk)

DOI: 10.4324/9781003358633

Typeset in Bembo MT Pro
by KnowledgeWorks Global Ltd.

Contents

Acknowledgements

We give special thanks to our teacher friends who gave us valuable insights on how to develop our work. In particular, we would like to thank Sue Davis, Linda Evans, Stewart Scott and Theo Whitworth.

Part I Theoretical and pedagogical perspectives

The power of rhymes and stories and your role in bringing them to life

Introduction

This book contains a personal selection of rhymes and stories to sing, chant or use in any way you wish with babies and young children. Part I is made up of three chapters. Together, they draw on some of the theories that underpin this oral, playful approach to learning, and you can use these chapters to help you to develop a rationale for your approach to teaching. Chapter 1 introduces readers to the ideas behind this book and discusses ways of supporting groups of children and individuals as they develop a love of rhyme, rhythm and story, leading to an understanding of early reading and the more formal and literary uses of language. In particular, it suggests ways of working with families and the wider community to support rhyming and storytelling across cultures and communities, including new arrivals who are in the process of learning English. Chapter 2 focuses on the way that stories and rhymes are crucial for the development of young children. Chapter 3 offers a wealth of advice on sharing rhymes and stories. Part II of the book is a resource bank. It contains a series of practical chapters, each with a selection of rhymes and traditional stories based around a particular theme and offers suggestions for using these rhymes and stories and developing response with the children you work with.

How to use this book

How you use this book will depend on your circumstances. You might be a busy trainee or a newly qualified teacher, for example, who is planning a session for young children with rhymes and stories. In such a case, we recommend that you go straight to Part II and develop some of the ideas in one of the chapters, as appropriate.

DOI: 10.4324/9781003358633-2

We encourage you to evaluate the session and adapt subsequent chapters accordingly. We envisage that teachers might begin with one particular story chapter in Part II and recite the rhymes, tell the story and adopt some of the suggested activities. You might use the chapter to stimulate your teaching. Thereafter, building on insights gained from evaluation and reflection, we hope that you will plan your own rhyming and story sessions in response to children's interests and prevailing circumstances.

Alternatively, you might be an early years leader who is planning a literacy workshop for parents, or developing the literacy policy, and need some theoretical content to back up the use of rhymes and stories. In such cases, we recommend you study one or more chapters in Part I of the book first so that you can point to the research behind such an approach.

This book is not a comprehensive resource. It cannot, for example, provide the detail needed by teachers of children with multiple and profound learning disabilities. However, we hope that teachers of *all* children, including children who rely solely on sensory experiences and who cannot access or communicate through language, will feel free to adapt and add to the ideas contained in this book. You will know the learning needs of the children you work with best. It is our hope that you will feel inspired to work with these ideas and adapt them to suit your children.

How did the book come about?

Sarah grew up in Argentina in a musical family steeped in songs, stories and rhythms. Her mother and father sang together, and the family frequently performed songs and shows to friends and their local communities. Sarah's father recited poems by heart to her as she went to sleep. He was an expert puppeteer and captivated children's attention with his Punch and Judy shows, with papier mâché puppets beautifully robed by Sarah's mother. It was in this "musical culture" (Malloch and Trevarthen, 2018) that Sarah's sense of rhythm and harmony and love for story were encouraged and strengthened. In England, Sarah worked for many years as an early years teacher. During this time, she built a collection of rhymes and songs to match children's interests and echo the seasons and festivals of the year. She kept each rhyme or song on a card in a box so that she could select which ones to use with the children. The box became a bank of well-loved, much repeated rhymes and songs.

Many years later, when Sarah worked at the University of Warwick, she met Hilary and mentioned the box to her. Hilary had for many years been a primary teacher and headteacher who loved teaching through stories. At Warwick, she taught a study module entitled Stories and Storytelling to her students. Sarah recited one of the rhymes from the box to her friend. Hilary immediately made the connection with a familiar story, and so the idea for this book came into being.

Why is this book relevant?

Rhymes and stories are considered important for young children's development and included in national curricula. For example, in the new Reading Framework in England, teachers are advised to

> identify a core set of poems…including rhyming poems, poems where alliteration is a strong feature, word games, traditional songs and rhymes, nonsense rhymes, and poems that are particularly rhythmical.
>
> (DfE, 2021, p .37)

The Early Years Foundation Stage in England (DfE, 2021) also promotes the use of poems and rhymes:

> Reading frequently to children, and engaging them actively in stories, non-fiction, rhymes and poems, and then providing them with extensive opportunities to use and embed new words in a range of contexts, will give children the opportunity to thrive.
>
> (DfE, 2021, p. 8)

The Te Whariki curriculum in New Zealand (Ministry of Education, 2017) promotes a language-rich environment for the youngest children, including familiar rhymes and songs.

In Part II of the book, a selection of rhymes and stories are included with practical ideas of how to work with them. The suggestions are open ended and designed to empower you to develop your own approach in relation to the children you work with. We encourage you to establish warm, regular opportunities for sharing rhymes and stories as you build relationships with the children and their families.

Who is this book written for?

This book is for everyone who works with, or has particular responsibility for, babies and early years children in nursery and primary school settings: early years teachers, nursery nurses, classroom assistants, childminders, parents, grandparents, nannies, playgroup leaders, foster parents, lunchtime supervisors and so on. The contents will also be of value to university students who are working towards early years degree courses.

To simplify matters, we refer to all those who support young children as teachers. We have taken the lead from June O'Sullivan, the early years social entrepreneur, who has argued for the use of the word teacher to refer to all who support young children, whatever their official title, since they all engage in "leading children to learn." As O'Sullivan (2022) argues:

> Teaching is how we respond, care and partner with the children to build their knowledge, understanding, capabilities and confidence in a way that meets their individual needs and idiosyncrasies. In doing so, this extends their learning and strengthens their cultural capital to ensure they achieve their potential. So, why not just use the word we all understand – and that's 'teacher'?
>
> (O'Sullivan, 2022)

We have therefore decided that you, the reader, whatever your role with young children and by virtue of the fact that you are reading this book, are a teacher. You are someone, we believe, who is committed to lifelong learning. You want to find out more so that you can support young children in the best way possible. As Cousins and Cunnah (2019) propose, you have a vocation to engage in this often complex work.

Why are rhymes and stories combined in this book?

Children learn from repeated rhymes, whether meaningful or nonsensical. They absorb the rhythms and sounds they hear. This is because they delight in the sounds of words and quickly begin to incorporate and adapt these rhythms and sounds to match their own word play. Repeated phrases in oral rhymes, such as "*Rap-a-tap-a-tap-a-tap, a tick-a-tack-a-too*" are easy-to-learn, "catchy" and enjoyable to say. Children are also drawn to stories. The stories in this book contain words or phrases that have a rhythmic pattern of their own ("*Not I*" *said the Cat … And so they pulled … and pulled … and pulled…*). Repeated phrases like these help children to remember the story and the words the characters use when they speak to each other.

These two fundamental, cultural forms of expression – traditional rhymes and stories – are brought together in this book to inspire you to develop both in tandem. Many of these rhymes are traditional; you might recognise them from your own childhood. A few of them have been written specifically by the authors to chime with a particular theme in the linking story. The authors have re-told their own versions of nine of the stories in Part II. One story, The Monkeys and the Crocodile, will be new to you, but you will find within it echoes of The Three Billy Goats Gruff. It is hoped that one rhyme will lead to a story and a story will suggest another rhyme and so on. We want you to have the freedom to choose which rhymes, stories, activities and techniques to draw on so that you can feel confident and motivated to share your own chosen rhymes and stories with an individual child or a group of children.

You might initially feel that some of the stories are perhaps too complicated or sophisticated for the young, but we have taken the decision to include them here because, in addition to forming a link with the main theme of each chapter, they are interesting and challenging in their own right. Crucially, we have found that teachers who tell these stories orally *without using a book to read from* usually find that young children can understand concepts and ideas that might otherwise elude them. This is because when you tell a story out of your mouth, using your own words, gestures and facial expressions, you can control the pace of the storytelling and encourage the children to take on the role of listener as you share eye contact with them, helping them to make sense of the story. We will say more about your role as a storyteller in Chapter 3.

The intention is that such an approach will inspire those of you who work closely with young children, so you can draw on your own and the children's experiences in diverse and international contexts and have the confidence to introduce a wide range of rhymes and stories from across the world.

Not all children have the same opportunities to hear rhymes and stories at home. We hope that the ideas in this book will be an encouragement to share them with parents and other family members, so they can use their favourite rhymes and stories at bedtime with their own children.

Parents, grandparents and other carers might have their own songs, poems and stories from their own childhood and cultures, and you are in an excellent position to invite them into your setting to share their favourite ones with the children. Accordingly, they can form part of your storytelling adventure alongside the children. Mary Medlicott's work with families over the years has shown her that:

> Reaching out beyond the setting is a vital aspect in the development of an effective story strategy…How any particular child will respond has, of course, much to do with their parents or carers. Living in a home where there are no books will have a big and largely negative impact on their general education. It will diminish the child's capacity for absorbing language and new ideas, let alone diminish her or his abilities in regard to learning to read.
>
> (Medlicott, 2018, p. 17)

The activities we propose in Part II offer a range of ideas for bringing teachers, parents and children together to experience rhymes and stories, and we hope that you will invite children's family members to visit your nursery, classroom or childcare setting, thereby helping children feel an increased sense of belonging. Such creative and inclusive approaches will inevitably expand the children's diet of rhymes and stories to set alight their literary development. Trevarthen understands this well:

> By making joint narratives, adults and infants come to share their history and invoke ideas from the community.
>
> (2013 p. 7)

Your role in supporting children's early literacy

The authors of this book recognise the devoted work that you do. You observe children closely and build up relationships with them and their families. You intervene sensitively and subtly to build on what children already know and help them take the next steps in their learning. You know when to call on the expertise of other professionals to support the children in your care. Over time, you will learn what works best with individual children and become adept at responding to children's own ideas for play in sensitive and creative ways. Thus, the suggestions in this book are not intended to dictate practice or override your own ideas and spontaneous responses to children's play. Rather, they are offered in a spirit of collaboration and respect, simply as a further set of ideas to develop and adapt as appropriate.

In nurseries and schools, particular people assigned to particular children, or "key persons" as they are known in England, know of the importance of building strong relationships of respect and trust with the children and families they serve. Similarly, in home contexts, childminders, foster parents or family members share this commitment to get to know children and learn what works best for them. Accordingly, it is anticipated that you will dip in and out of this book when you find particular rhymes, stories and activities helpful. You might be following children's particular interests, such as growing seeds, or noticing a particular season of the year or talking about the importance of helping each other; wider contexts like this give young children an opportunity to think about broader issues that concern them, set within the context of a rhyme and story. At the beginning of each rhyme and story chapter, you will find a set of overriding themes to help you navigate the book and make these links.

Supporting children who speak English as an additional language

Children in nurseries and early years classrooms across the country reflect the multicultural and multilingual nature of our society. Increasing numbers of children worldwide speak two or more languages. For some, their experience of English will inevitably be limited for a time. However, as Daniel (2012) discovered, through rhyming and storying, these children can be encouraged to hear "models of language which are comprehensible but also beyond what the learners are able to produce themselves" (p. 66). In other words, children benefit from hearing and reciting rhymes with repetition and rhythm, whether or not they understand their meaning. Repeating rhymes as part of their play supports language development.

The rhymes and stories you share and repeat with these young learners will therefore help them to absorb the language in an enjoyable way. Indeed, children who are learning English benefit enormously from listening to the kind of rhymes and stories in this book because they are invited to hear the sounds and the rhythmic patterned structure of the English language. As they tune in to the "melody" of the language and structure of stories, they will grow in confidence and begin to join in with rhyming and storytelling. Margaret Meek knew the value of using patterned rhymes and stories:

> Pupils in the process of learning English seem to benefit most from internalising the typical rhythms and cadences of different types of discourse…in stories told or read to them.
>
> (Meek, 1996, p. 60)

Children learn through repetition and patterns. As you establish a regular rhyming and storytelling approach to your teaching, so you will help children to participate in these shared experiences. Bligh and Drury (2015) discovered, in their ethnographic research, that young bilingual learners benefited through such opportunities to join in with others. The researchers concluded that "learning takes place within and through participation with others who model practices to be learned" (p. 272). Do not, therefore, be afraid to repeat stories and rhymes as long as the children enjoy them. Develop rituals and practices, with props and actions as needed. Allow bilingual learners opportunities to repeat language and join in with others. Such opportunities to participate will support rich and rapid language acquisition.

Supporting new arrivals to feel a sense of belonging

Sarah recently worked with a bilingual advocate to support a small group of Afghan refugee children. She taught them the Rap-a-tap-a-rap-a-tap rhyme. They were all seated on the floor, or near to the ground, and took as long as they needed to explore the sounds and movements of the rhyme. There were no time restraints on the activity. The children responded with enthusiasm and enjoyment.

Sarah observed that the repeating phrase *Rap-a-tap-a-rap-a-tap* was easy for the children to catch on to, necessitating distinct and contrasting mouth shapes as the lips joined up on the "p" sound and moved backwards and forwards to the top of the mouth for the "t" sound. Sarah showed the children a small hammer to help the children to understand the meaning of the word "hammerman" and to facilitate understanding of how he was performing the action. The children wanted to manipulate this, and Sarah supervised them as they held it safely and mimed the hammering actions. Sarah noticed that *"the busy little hammerman"* phrase encouraged a pleasing alliteration of the "m" sound.

The only prerequisites were careful planning, the courage to improvise and be creative and an appreciation of language. We have used this example to illustrate how a simple repetitive rhyme can be used to support children who are new to the English language. It is pleasing to think that the rhythms of this phrase will stay with the children even though they might not yet fully understand the meaning.

One of the stories in this book, The Flying Tortoise, is based on an Indian folk tale told to Hilary by one of the parents of the children in her school. As you build a community of mutual respect and trust with the families you serve, so you will encourage them to share favourite stories and rhymes in their own languages. These shared experiences will thus be enriched and expanded through these cultural exchanges. Indeed, as Harold Rosen (1993) reminded us:

> If the culture of the community is to enter the culture of the school, its stories must come too and, more profoundly perhaps, its oral storytelling traditions must become an acknowledged form of making meaning.
>
> (Rosen, 1993, p. 27)

Parkinson (2011) too proposed that:

> Traditional stories often reflect the accumulated wisdom of generations. This is why they are passed on: they mean something important.
>
> (p. 5)

This exchange of stories, we suggest, is crucially important. We therefore encourage you to enjoy the stories and rhymes in this book and have the courage to adapt them so that you make each story your own and re-shape it to reflect your young audience and the community in which you live. Using stories from your own life together with the stories the children bring into the classroom setting will help you to create new, joint narratives and provide you with a set of stories that are unique to your setting. Such an approach supports emotional development too. Mary Medlicott has long argued that "story is a journey of the emotions," so even if a young child understands very little English, she observed that the child "can experience the emotions of the story through the tones of voice in which it's conveyed. The journey of the story," Medlicott continues, "gives the experience of a beginning and an end and something that happens in between. This is satisfying" (2018, p. 68).

This growing sense of story structure will inevitably help children to develop an understanding of the direction of a story; perhaps more significantly, this journey of the emotions enlarges young children's ability to feel compassion for others and to engage with their fears and joys. And this is why children feel happy for The Sleeping Beauty when she awakens from her long sleep and afraid for Goldilocks when she breaks Baby Bear's chair. This aspect of fear will be discussed later in this chapter.

Supporting children with special educational needs and disabilities

You will work particularly closely with families and other professionals to support children with special educational needs and disabilities (SEND). These family members and professionals will know what works best for the children they care for. For example, they could suggest that a child with hearing loss may enjoy feeling the vibrations of a percussion instrument played to the rhythm of the rhyme. By adopting an inclusive approach, you will be considering the individual needs of each child, including their likes and dislikes. For these children with SEND, sensory experiences are particularly important for their development and learning (Borkett, 2021). Inviting them to feel the wind in their hair (Wind and Sun), taste bread (Baking Bread), watch plants grow (Growing Things) and listen out for quiet sounds (Hungry Little Mice) will certainly help these children to develop and learn through sensory stimulus.

Sometimes we need to develop particular strategies to use with individual children using all our professional expertise. Mary Medlicott has written movingly about her encounter with a four-year-old girl with special needs who screamed loudly and tried to get away when Mary told her story. But when Mary introduced a little tune into the story, the little girl "stopped mid-stream and briefly gave me her full attention." Mary sang this little song throughout the story and observed that once again the girl listened. Mary writes that "I suddenly realised I now had a simple song which, miraculously, could be repeated over and over …. Each time I used it, the girl would listen" (Medlicott, 2006, p. 35). It seems that the song had a calming effect on her and perhaps gave her the confidence to respond to Mary, who was now no longer a stranger. Every child is different. As you get to know your children, you will develop your own approach with them. You might find that particular songs, playful rhymes or repeated activities soothe them.

Choosing rhymes and stories from diverse cultures and contexts

We have already suggested that you can invite people from your local community to take part in rhyme and story sessions. Vivian Gussin Paley (1990) reminds us that "the storyteller is a 'culture builder'" (p. 34) and she explains why it is valuable for children to experience stories from different cultures and contexts. Each culture has its own rich tradition of rhymes and stories, and though it obviously takes some careful organisation, an invitation to local people – librarians, butchers, shopkeepers and hairdressers – enriches the literary diet of the school or nursery setting, and it not only leads to greater understanding of a range of cultures and contexts but also allows everyone in the community to feel valued and respected. The Reading Framework (DfE, 2021) in England recommends that children should "learn about the lives of those whose experiences and perspectives differ from their own" and that "choosing stories and non-fiction that explore such differences begins to break down a sense of otherness that often leads to division and prejudice" (p. 28). Similarly, the Early Years Foundation Stage (DfE, 2021) in England stipulates that "listening to a broad selection of stories, non-fiction, rhymes and poems will foster [children's] understanding of our culturally, socially, technologically and ecologically diverse world" (p. 10).

Julia Donaldson, author of the well-loved The Gruffalo (1999), argues that "stories should be universal, so if there is a message, it should be for anyone at any time" (The Guardian, 3 September 2022). Some of the rhymes and stories in this book are fantastical, outmoded or archaic. Nevertheless, the rhythms, patterns, messages and values they contain are timeless and relevant to all children, irrespective of their culture or background, because they are based on elemental themes that resonate with every child's experience, forming a bridge between the world of home, school and community and the children's own private inner world of feeling.

On the value of fairy tales

Fairy tales migrate on soft feet, for borders are invisible to them, no matter how ferociously they are policed by cultural purists.

(Warner, 2014, p. XV)

Warner understands the value of these wonderful stories which have existed for as long as groups of people have felt the need to share their own wisdom and truth. The stories in this book are either traditional fairy tales re-told or contain echoes of fairy tales, with their traditional patterns and elements of magic and magical people, elves and trolls and animals that can talk. The range and breadth of them cannot be measured or contained in any human database (Warner, 2014). They are a special and important form of literature and, we hold, crucial to young children's development. We have tried to maintain a balance between the selection of stories and rhymes that use people as the main characters and those where animals play the central role because we know that some will appeal to particular children more than others. But all the rhymes and stories in Part II of this book, irrespective of whether their emphasis is on animals or humans, contain elemental features that are instantly recognisable to young readers and listeners. These aspects allow them to experience a complex and intense range of personal emotions as they share in the despair and then the delight of the shoemaker and his wife or the vulnerability and ordeal of big green turtle as he finds himself flying through the air when he opens his mouth and loses his grip on the stick.

All the rhymes and stories in this book contain rich imagery designed to grip a child's imagination, inviting them to enter new worlds, speculate about what the characters do and relate things that happen in their own lives. These ideas will be stored in children's memories. Goddard Blythe, who has worked with young children for many years, is convinced that rhymes and stories nurture children. She has observed that:

> Old fairy tales often speak intuitively and imaginatively to the child's experience, developmental stages, fears and concerns.
>
> (Goddard Blythe, 2011, p. 131)

Warner (2014) has identified five defining characteristics of fairy tales. Firstly, fairy tales are short narratives; secondly, they are familiar stories or stories that children are likely to have heard before in some form or other. Thirdly, fairy tales contain familiar features. Their characters, plots, special objects or powers may have appeared in other stories, and this set of intertextual links helps children because, as Julia Kristeva argued in the 1960s, no story is original – everything is borrowed from other literary works. This understanding, while it can never be articulated or explicitly understood by children, nevertheless helps them to make subtle links between characters, events and authorial style; this is why some children can make the connection between the three bears who appear in The Jolly Postman (Ahlberg and Ahlberg, 1986) and the bears in the traditional Goldilocks story – a textual skill that will be of enormous value to young learners as they develop more sophisticated reading techniques and learn to carry meaning from one story to another (Minns, 1997, p. 122). Fourthly, according to Warner (2014), fairy tales use symbols to tell stories as they are, no more or less. They are not altered to make the outcomes somehow more palatable or bearable. Finally, fairy tales contain supernatural elements. Things can be fixed or occur by magic. They thus evoke a combination of pleasure and wonder, as children begin to imagine dragons or wizards and all kinds of magical monsters that form part of our storytelling worlds and help them to find a satisfying meaning in stories they read and listen to.

Choosing stories with troubling features and endings

The rhymes and stories in this collection contain many of these defining characteristics. For example, they tell the stories as they are. Therefore, in some cases, you will find that things do not go well for the characters involved and some things happen to them that are frightening. In the story of The Monkeys and the Crocodile, for example, Teeny-Tiny Monkey and his mother and father are almost eaten by the crocodile. You may feel understandably anxious about sharing stories that contain frightening episodes – even death, and early years teachers often avoid choosing these particular rhymes and stories and instead substitute "safe" stories. But John Yorke (2014) proposed that, if there is nothing shocking in the stories themselves, then they are likely to contain limited allure. Stories, he argued, are more engaging if they include

> rough edges, the darkness – and we love these things because though we may not consciously want to admit it, they touch something deep inside us.
>
> (Yorke, 2014, p. 14)

Yorke suggested that listeners or readers are swept into stories when, somehow, they tap into their unconscious, horrify them or connect with their own unspoken fears. We believe Yorke is right to suggest that frightening feelings can even be enjoyed, particularly if they are shared with an audience of young listeners who as a group can experience the power of these scary emotions. Thus, we can see how stories play both a social and emotional role in children's development and understanding. Will Storr (2020) also emphasised the importance of struggle and obstacles in stories. In The Monkeys and the Crocodile story, the monkey family must enter the river, face the crocodile and get to the other side. These opposing forces of good and evil are a signature feature of stories. Indeed, it is through encountering difficulties that protagonists learn and change. The crocodile in the rhyme The Swampy River Crocodile shows us that he has a soft side, and this revelation helps young listeners to foster compassion and humanity.

But are we right to share stories with troubling features and endings with children? Clearly, no-one wants the children in their setting to experience fear and to have nightmares about certain situations they meet in rhymes and stories, but, on the other hand, perhaps we underestimate children's resilience. Some professional storytellers with many years of experience argue that we should not be afraid of helping children to face and to overcome their fears. As Betty Rosen (1991) said:

> I believe very strongly that as teachers our main sin is to underestimate the perceptions of children. They can respond to more than we allow them.
>
> (p. 32)

Perhaps the key word here is "respond": if we choose to share rhymes and stories that contain fearsome things, then we need to give children time to absorb these issues and to talk about difficult issues if they wish. This is surely part of our responsibility to the young. The giants, monsters, dragons and trolls that children meet in fairy stories are metaphors for everything that is dark, unknown and beyond their control. Fairy stories translate these fears into images and give them names, allowing children to gain entry to dark places while at the same time helping them to step outside everything that is fearful and scary and to view the dragons and trolls in their minds from a place of safety.

It is the same when we find pleasure and joy at the end of a story; the metaphors resonate with the child listener or reader, and this feeling of delight can engender a lifelong love of story and language. This is why many stories end with the image of being tucked up in bed by a loving parent or having tea together with friends and family. You might recall the ending of that very special and indispensable book, *Where The Wild Things Are* by Maurice Sendak (1967). After Max has said goodbye to the Wild Things, he returns to his bedroom "where he found his supper waiting for him … and it was still hot." Despite his rage at being sent to his room for his destructive behaviour, his mother still loves and cherishes him and always will.

Trisha Lee (2016), whose seminal work has grown out of the Helicopter stories of Vivian Gussin Paley, has also considered this matter closely:

> Story has the ability to connect us with the emotions of a character, whilst at the same time distancing us from the personal aspects of our own circumstances. Knowing that good overcomes evil can help us face things that feel difficult or unfair in our own lives. Metaphor allows us to explore these issues safely.
>
> (p. 71)

Many children will be familiar with The Snowman by Raymond Briggs, either through reading the book itself or by watching the animated television film. The boy in the story, who builds the snowman and flies with him through the night sky, wakes up the next morning to find his snowman has melted. "I don't have happy endings," Briggs explained in a Radio Times interview in 2012.

> I create what seems natural and inevitable. The snowman melts, my parents died, animals die, flowers die. Everything dies. There's nothing particularly gloomy about it. It's a fact of life.
>
> (Lea, 2022)

Children have their own way of dealing with this sense of loss. A young boy whom Donald Fry (1985) studied told him that when he read The Snowman: "I don't look at the last page … I always turn it over to the white, to the white pages and then go back" (p. 19) – back to the beginning, that is, to re-create the story all over again, returning to the joy of watching the little boy playing in the snow and building the snowman. Bob Barton and David Booth, both professional storytellers, have thought about the matter of love and loss for many years. They explain:

> We are not saying that all stories should end happily, but they need to offer hope to young people and encourage them to overcome difficulties and stand up to wrongdoing. In the story, the dog may die but there must be a puppy… The context of 'long ago' enables children to explore a variety of problems and concerns that have troubled humanity forever, but in a safe, non-threatening framework.
>
> (Booth and Barton, 2000, p. 19)

In the end, of course, the decision about whether or not to include dark tales is yours but we would argue that stories like The Monkeys and the Crocodiles and Precious Toys and Playthings give young children a chance to explore, in symbolic form, the trials and wonders of life, with its many delights, challenges, problems and dangers, all experienced safely inside a story.

So, on the one hand, it is vital for children to encounter challenges, disasters and fears in stories, as they will in life. At the same time, it is important to distinguish the story from reality, such as setting it in a distant time or place, and to offer a hopeful outcome, such as new growth or life.

On the use of archaic language

Rhymes and stories help children to become familiar with a variety of literary words, phrases, language patterns and sentences used in written, as well as spoken, language. Some of the rhymes and stories in this book are highly literary and include outmoded and old-fashioned expressions and words. You might observe that the children find some of these words and phrases rather unusual. However, we have decided not to modernise these texts or translate them into current forms of expression. Instead, and in order to address this issue, each story chapter contains a glossary of the more unusual rhyme and story words. You can use the glossary in whatever way you find useful.

It is noticeable that The Reading Framework (DfE, 2021) in England focuses on the important relationship between talk and stories, and "the role stories play in developing young children's vocabulary and language"; of particular significance are "words that children would rarely hear or use in everyday speech" (p. 7). We suggest that the use of unfamiliar words and phrases *within* stories and rhymes helps young listeners to take a calculated guess at the meaning, an important reading lesson that gives young learners an opportunity to make predictions. And so, they have an opportunity, guided by your discussion, to expand their lexical knowledge, predict the meaning of uncommon words and learn how these words fit into a larger phrase or sentence.

Some of the quaint rhyming chants in the stories in this book will be unfamiliar to young listeners who have never met rhymes before. Children enjoy repeating story refrains and rhymes, whether or not they understand them, are in their own language or have any reference to their worlds. You might have to exercise patience and be prepared to repeat the chant over and over again, until children feel comfortable with the sounds. For example, children who have never listened to, or joined in with the story of The Three Billy Goats Gruff, will certainly never have heard:

Who's that trip-trapping over my bridge?

This matters because chants like this allow children to play with language and make The Three Billy Goats Gruff a story that they will remember. The rhythmic patterning of the chant (and of course many other chants of a similar nature in other well-known tales) is essential to the flow of the story.

Rhymes and stories such as The Three Billy Goats Gruff have license to include nonsensical phrases, confer magic and allow events to occur that would not normally occur. These chants are invariably passed on orally, and we hope you will adapt them to match the needs of your young listeners. They serve to *entertain* more than to inform, to give pleasure rather than lead to deep reflection and to create a new world rather than replicate the everyday world. In practical terms, they give children a chance to join in your story and they will certainly encourage their awareness of language as well as conferring a sense of solidarity and belonging.

We therefore encourage you to include these repetitive, rhythmic features when you share rhymes and stories. We hope that the distinct rhythms and structures contained in this book will support you to do this.

And so, we encourage you to adopt this rhyming, storying approach with the children you care for. Begin with stories or rhymes you know well, or dip into this book for ideas about how to make a start. In the next chapter, we give you a rationale for adopting such an approach. We draw on theories of child development to support this way of teaching.

References

Ahlberg, A. & Ahlberg, J. (1986), *The Jolly Postman or Other People's Letters*. London: Heinemann.

Bligh, C. & Drury, R. (2015), 'Perspectives on the "Silent Period" for Emergent Bilinguals in England', *Journal of Research in Childhood Education*, 29(2), pp. 259–274. doi:10.1080/02568543.2015.1009589. [22 July 2022]

Booth, D. & Barton, B. (2000), *Story Works: How Teachers Can Use Shared Stories in the New Curriculum, Pembroke*, Markham: Ontario.

Borkett, P. (2021), *Special Educational Needs in the Early Years: A Guide to Inclusive Practice*, London: Sage.

Cousins, S. & Cunnah, W. (2018), *Investigating Emotional, Sensory and Social Learning in Early Years Practice*, London: Routledge.

Daniel, A.K. (2012), *Storytelling Across the Curriculum*, London and New York: Routledge.

Department for Education (DfE). (2021), Statutory Framework for the Early Years Foundation Stage Setting the Standards for Learning, Development and Care for Children from Birth to Five, https://www.gov.uk/government/publications

Department for Education (DfE). (2021), The Reading Framework: Teaching the Foundations of Literacy. Guidance for Schools to Meet Existing Expectations for Teaching Early Reading.

Donaldson, J. & Scheffler, A. (1999), *The Gruffalo*, London: Macmillan Children's Books.

Fry, D. (1985), *Children Talk About Books: Seeing Themselves as Readers*, Open University Press: Milton Keynes.

Goddard Blythe, S. (2011), *The Genius of Natural Childhood: Secrets of Thriving Children*, Early Years Series, Stroud: Hawthorn Press.

Lea, R. (2022), Snowman author Raymond Briggs dies aged 88, https://www.theguardian.com/books/2022/aug/10/snowman-author-raymond-briggs-dies-aged-88

Lee, T. (2016), *Princesses, Dragons and Helicopter Stories: Storytelling and Story Acting in the Early Years*, London and New York: Routledge.

Malloch, S. & Trevarthen, C. (2018), 'The Human Nature of Music', *Frontiers in Psychology*, 9. doi: 10.3389/fpsyg.2018.01680. [20 February 2021].

Medlicott, M. (2006), *Tell It: A Practical Guide to Storytelling with Children Across the Primary Age-Range*, a storyworks publication.

Medlicott, M. (2018), *Storytelling and Story-Reading in Early Years: How to Tell and Read Stories to Young Children*, London: Jessica Kingsley.

Meek, M. (1996), *Developing Pedagogies in the Multilingual Classroom: The Writings of Josie Levine*, Stoke-on-Trent: Trentham.

Ministry of Education, New Zealand. (2017), Te Whāriki – Early childhood curriculum, www.education.govt.nz

Minns, H. (1997), *Read It to Me Now! Learning at Home and at School*. Buckingham: Open University Press.

O'Sullivan, J. (2022), 'Let's Hear It for the Early Years Teacher', June O'Sullivan's blog posted on 28 June 2022, https://leyf.org.uk/early-years-teachers/

Paley, V.G. (1990), *The Boy Who Would be a Helicopter: the Uses of Storytelling in the Classroom*, Cambridge, Mass. and London: Harvard University Press.

Parkinson, R. (2011), *Storytelling and Imagination: Beyond Basic Literacy 8–14*, London and New York: Routledge.

Rosen, B. (1991), *"Is My Story Too Frightening?" in Shapers and Polishers: Teachers as Storytellers*, London: Mary Glasgow.

Rosen, H. (1993), *Stories and Meanings*, Sheffield: National Association for the Teaching of English.

Sendak, M. (1967), *Where The Wild Things Are*. London: The Bodley Head.

Storr, W. (2020), *The Science of Storytelling: Why Stories Make Us Human and How to Tell Them Better*, New York, NY: Abrams, Inc. Available from: ProQuest Ebook Central [6 September 2022].

Trevarthen, C. (2013), 'What Young Children Know About Living and Learning With Companions', *Nordisk Barnehageforskning*, 6. doi: 10.7577/nbf.441.

Warner, M. (2014), *Once upon a Time: A Short History of Fairy Tale*, Oxford: Oxford University Press, Incorporated. Available from: ProQuest Ebook Central [15 November 2022].

Yorke, J. (2014), Into the Woods: A Five Act Journey into Story, VLE Books [6 September 2022].

2 The importance of rhymes and stories for children's learning and development

We agree with Gordon Wells' argument that "stories have a role in education that goes far beyond their contribution to the acquisition of literacy" (1986, p. 194), and it is important to note from the start that this is not a book directly aimed at helping children learn to read. Our intention has not been to prepare children for school nor to see rhymes and stories as a necessary precursor to reading and writing. Instead, we see such experiences as being valuable in their own right. Children absorb the rhythms, sounds and patterns of repeated rhymes and stories, as well as the mood and suspense found in oral folk tales, and these elements form the basis of children's enjoyment of rhymes and stories in the early years. Having said that, we need to bear in mind Margaret Meek's important observation that "reading does not happen in a vacuum" (1988, p. 6). Rather, young readers draw on their layered experience of language, story, and song as they set out on the road to becoming literate, and in this respect, our book is very much a part of children's early literacy experience, so we advocate making links between children's learning and development and the rhyming, storying approach we offer here. However, we insist that such an approach does so much more than prepare children for school or lead to healthy development. Principally, it provides opportunities for children and adults to enjoy their time together and to be creative, thereby bringing happiness and leading to a sense of well-being. Such positive moments have lifelong effects on children's lives.

In this chapter, we delve more deeply into the characteristics of rhymes and stories that make them indispensable for the emotional and intellectual growth of babies and young children. In particular, we analyse the ways in which the use of highly patterned language of rhymes and stories supports children's ability to create this kind of rhythmic and repetitive language for themselves, by extending their vocabulary and adding to their growing knowledge of the grammatical structures of the English language. We consider the significance of the musicality of chants and songs and

DOI: 10.4324/9781003358633-3

the importance of sharing the repeated phrases found in traditional stories, before discussing the social bond that is formed when children listen to stories as a group and are encouraged to share their own personal stories in a supportive and stimulating environment. These activities, we argue, help young children to develop imaginative insights into their own lives, both through their own narrative re-tellings and through their creation of imaginative drawings and paintings that help them re-present the world of the story. Finally, we suggest that the complex problems faced by characters in these rhymes and stories invite speculation and curiosity and form the basis of intellectual enquiry, reflective thinking and mathematical reasoning on the part of the children.

The rhymes and stories in this book are ones that the authors value themselves; they have not been selected at random. Many people who work with young children seem to have noticed that traditional rhymes and stories have been lost from the curriculum; this is regrettable since teachers who continue to use these timeless narratives understand that the best traditional tales and rhymes contain universal values, showing us a way to behave in our encounters with other people, how to help each other and how to learn what is important in our lives. Paley (1990) observes that "by the time most children are four they can identify and debate many of the issues hidden in these age-old plots" (p. 132). This is because these "age-old plots" help to increase children's consciousness by giving them a framework through which to discuss issues and to see alternative points of view. They begin to take on another's perspective as they are encouraged to develop an imaginative sympathy with the characters they meet in stories and rhymes. This intellectual and emotional journey helps them to attain personal growth. Adults who share traditional rhymes and stories with young children, whether at home or at school, rightly understand that narrative is indeed a powerful learning tool which embodies our cultural history.

Many of the stories we have selected are from the European tradition, but we have also included folk tales from other parts of the world because they too are part of our cultural heritage and will introduce children to new delights in the form of characters and events in a variety of different contexts. See, for example, the story of Ana in Precious Toys and Playthings. But irrespective of their origin, the stories we have included here teach children to think imaginatively about ideas, to be quiet and patient, to overcome obstacles in life, to be kind, to fight against injustice, to be truthful and to listen to the views of other people.

The traditional rhymes have been specifically chosen because they have been popular with the children Sarah taught. They contain catchy rhythms and phrases and are enjoyable to chant or sing together, and indeed, singing and repeating rhymes helps children feel a sense of belonging. Singing and chanting in unison is an enjoyable, reciprocal experience for teachers and family members who care for young children and who hold these rhymes deep in their own hearts. As Amanda Niland found in her narrative portrait research, babies and very young children are "naturally drawn to come together through singing" (2015, p. 14). Niland discovered that shared singing created "moments of togetherness" (2015, p. 14), thereby helping children develop a strong relationship and to feel a part of the group. You might remember particular rhymes yourselves as children and remember sharing them over and over again with a loved adult. Such rich, happy encounters and the comfortable and enjoyable feelings associated with children's early experiences of rhymes will remain with children throughout their lives.

It is no coincidence that rhymes and stories, both written and spoken, form the basis of young children's first experience of hearing the structural forms of written language. This is because this patterned language is based on what we might call the 3Rs – Rhyme, Rhythm and Repetition. These three important ingredients are present in the rhymes and the traditional stories in this book. They are particularly important because they help young children to feel the *pulse* of the rhyme or the repeated phrase. Some people associate this with hearing the comforting and familiar sound of their mother's heartbeat before birth. The musicality of the rhythms and the repeated phrases in the stories and rhymes in this book become ingrained in children's minds and help them to anticipate what is coming next, even if they don't fully understand the meaning of the words. This ability to predict gives them the confidence to remember the sequence of events, to take a guess at what might happen next and to join in with the words and actions.

Some children who enter early years settings will be familiar with more complex forms of written language because they will have been used to hearing stories and rhymes at home, but others come into the nursery or early years classroom with underdeveloped language skills. Those who have been lucky enough to listen to rhymes and stories from babyhood develop an "ear" for the way that written language is used and an interest in new vocabulary. "What does 'bleating' mean?" asked a four-year-old when he listened to his teacher reading him a story about a sheep (Minns, 1997, p. 93). Not only do stories and rhymes help children to develop a love of words and an interest in new vocabulary but they also help children to understand the kinds of literary phrases and sentences that we find in written language, such as "Once upon a time in a deep, dark wood..." or "Wee Willy Whiskers, Chinese Chopsticks." The structure of these words and phrases is very different from that found in everyday language we use at home, in the classroom and in the playground, surely a good preparation for learning to read and write.

Rhymes and stories to support language development and social interaction

The rhyming and storying approach we advocate supports important theories of language development and thought processes, which are closely aligned to the work of Lev Vygotsky and Jerome Bruner. Although neither of these powerful thinkers wrote directly about the value of rhymes and stories in early learning, many of their arguments support the teaching and learning of these elements in the early years. It is significant that Vygotsky argued that:

> Human learning presupposes a specific social nature and a process by which children grow into the intellectual life of those around them.
>
> (Vygotsky, 1978, p. 88)

All human learning, he argued, is dialogic, rather like a conversation, and he placed enormous value on the social exchanges of talk and shared activities, particularly between an experienced adult and less experienced children. This social interaction, he argued, stimulated learning in a variety of contexts. Vygotsky described this experience as the "zone of proximal development," indicating that it can be best described as

> the distance between the actual developmental level as determined by independent problem-solving and the level of potential development as determined through problem-solving under adult guidance or in collaboration with more capable peers.
>
> (Vygotsky, 1978, p. 86)

The psychologist Jerome Bruner was closely influenced by the theories of Vygotsky. His observations of young children in the process of learning led him to develop the notion of "scaffolding." In everyday terms, the experienced teacher gives the inexperienced learner as much learning support as is needed, gradually withdrawing this support as the child grows in understanding. Bruner and his colleagues describe the process in this way:

> This scaffolding consists essentially of the adult 'controlling' those elements of the task that are initially beyond the learner's capacity, thus permitting him to concentrate upon and complete only those elements that are within his range of competence.
>
> (Wood, Bruner and Ross, 1976, p. 90)

In a later book, Bruner wrote about an outstanding science teacher who taught him when he was about ten years old. She was explaining the movement of molecules and he remembers her:

> expressing a sense of wonder that matched, indeed bettered, the sense of wonder I felt at that age (around ten) about everything I turned my mind to…In effect, she was inviting me to extend my world of wonder to encompass hers. She was not just informing me. She was, rather, negotiating the world of wonder and possibility.
>
> (Bruner, 1976, p. 126)

You might be wondering what this has to do with the teaching and learning of rhymes and stories. We would say, everything. The transmission of knowledge, the excitement of new learning and the engagement of the teacher and the learner are rooted in the sharing of rhymes and stories in exactly the same way. Bruner's model of teaching and learning resonates powerfully for us because the co-operative learning we have in mind here and the nature of the shared activities we suggest in Part II of this book rely on your experience and competence as mediators of rhymes and stories that babies and young children would certainly be unable to access independently. The social interchanges between you and the children form a powerful learning bond between you, the experienced teacher, and the young children you are supporting. Indeed, we believe that the interchange of ideas that happens in rhyming and story-telling sessions encourages and develops co-operation and negotiation between you and the young children in your care.

Rhymes and stories for healthy brain development

There is no doubt that rhymes and stories extend children's own use of both written and spoken language. Young children who are exposed to this kind of patterned and elaborate literary language begin to internalise these more complex structures and use them confidently to generate their own rhymes and stories. This constant repetition of rhymes and chants fosters connections in children's brains, which are very plastic and are shaped by early experiences, as Conkbayir testifies:

> The changes that happen in the brain during these first tender years become the permanent foundation upon which all later brain function is built. For the brain's neural networks to develop normally during this sensitive period, a child needs responsive and timely input. For example, it is during face-to-face interactions that babies and children practise the art of conversation and build trust in their parents/caregivers.
>
> (Conkbayir, 2016)

Such enjoyable encounters, also known as "serve and return interactions" (Center of the Developing Child, Harvard University), help to shape brain architecture. When very young children make gestures or babble and you respond with your eyes, sounds or mouth movements, neural connections are formed and strengthened in their brains. This helps young children to develop their communication and social skills. The more enjoyable these backward and forward movements are, the more they will support children's development. We are convinced that these early, enjoyable and rich moments with others become permanent foundations for healthy development in many areas of learning, as we shall explore below.

Forming close attachments through shared songs, rhymes and stories

Teachers are understandably apprehensive when they are faced with a new group of children. Often, the best way of forming a bond with a new child or group is through sharing stories and rhymes. Children develop attachments to their storytellers. Indeed, as Trevarthen (2015) proposed, "the infant brain is primarily concerned with the receptive and expressive functions that arise through the intimate affective attachment, body to body, animated by love" (para 81). Children enjoy these rhyme and storytelling sessions when they are physically close to familiar companions they trust and love. These warm emotions remain with children for life and build up their resilience. Booth and Barton (2000) sum up this emotional and inclusive experience neatly:

> The coming together to hear stimulating material presented by an enthusiastic teller or reader resembles a ritual initiation which reinforces the idea that each and every human being is part of the total interconnectedness of things.
>
> (Barton and Booth, 2000, p. 30)

This bond, this communal sharing and listening, this interconnectedness, helps children to develop a strong sense of self, to experience moments of happiness and to feel cherished. These emotions remain ingrained in their beings and build up their emotional strength as they learn to navigate their own lives and identities.

The connection that is created between children and their teachers in nursery, classroom or home settings is crucially important. In some settings, children are encouraged to read stories on their own on a computer or tablet, but even though they clearly enjoy this activity, we would argue that they could be missing out on the one-to-one contact that a significant person would give them. Sensitive teachers are aware of this and make time to listen to children's responses and to interact with them, thus creating a bond through shared experience. Bob Barton and David Booth comment on the way that families have changed, citing in particular social mobility or family breakdown, and they remind us that:

> Story is a social process; we transform it as we tell it to fit the way we think. Our telling is shaped by everything in our life and our culture. We gain membership in our cultural community by telling stories.
>
> (Barton and Booth, 2000, p. 13)

It is the authors' belief that by listening to oral stories and rhymes children can share more deeply in the process of creation – and we are often surprised when we realise how creative these children can be. Four-year-old Jane and Tejinder play together with magical figurines on the magnet board. Jane asks Tejinder why she has put a dragon on the board, and this is Tejinder's explanation:

> We want the dragon on to kill the witch, don't we? Cos that's a nice little fairy and she wouldn't hurt the witch would she? Cos she's got to fly away from the witch hasn't she? Cos she didn't want to get hurt would she? She didn't know there was a witch on there did she?

Tejinder's explanation shows the potential of this kind of collaborative talk. Paley (1990) would probably call Tejinder's explanation "an exercise in logic" (p. 97). She explores this process further:

> Problems are not meant to be solved. They are ours to practice on, to explore the possibilities with, to help us study cause and effect.
>
> (Paley, 1990, p. 80)

Paley would surely agree that, like Tejinder and Jane, the process of listening and making mental images helps children to see objects, people and places in their mind's eye as they bring their experience to bear on what the storyteller has told them. "Baby bear's bed is dead cosy," says four-year-old Ranu. "Just like mine." Ranu is seeing herself inside the story of Goldilocks and the Three Bears, and she is busy organising her thoughts within the framework of the plot.

Music, rhyme and rhythm: developing an "ear" for sounds and chants

Singing, chanting and responding to musical sound effects of all kinds go hand in hand with the sharing and transmission of rhymes and stories right across the world, and so, it is no coincidence that we have used musical terms such as "rhythm," "tone," "musicality of the language" and "refrain" to discuss the way in which the textual language of rhyme and story uses these components almost as second nature. Percy Scholes (1970), author of The Oxford Companion to Music, has even suggested that there is "an imaginary metronome that seems to form part of the mental equipment of every human being" (p. 874).

Children join the world within a particular "musical culture" (Malloch and Trevarthen, 2018) and engage in cultural exchanges from birth. All children, not just those who are born into musical families, experience musicality since "everywhere mothers and fathers speak with a musical intonation to their young infants" (Trevarthen, 2013, p. 3). Parents and other key attachment figures move, speak and sing in their own unique ways and these become children's musical cultures, so hearing "the tune on the page" becomes a part of their language repertoire. David Crystal (1987), coming at this from the perspective of a linguist, describes intonation in speech as its "melody" or "music" (p. 173).

Music is everywhere, and musicality is within everyone. Indeed, as proposed by Malloch and Trevarthen, children have an innate musicality and "music is at the centre of what it means to be human" (2018, p. 1). You, or other "loving caregivers," are ideally suited to encourage and build on this musicality (2018, p. 1). Music can help to establish a sense of companionship. Babies and very young children become attuned to the "musical intonation" (Trevarthen, 2013, p. 3) and the ways of moving, speaking and singing of their parents and other family members.

Children who listen to traditional rhymes and stories soon become familiar with the distinctive rhythms and patterned structures they hear over and over again; for example, *Three little kittens, they lost their mittens, And they began to cry.* Given encouragement, children soon begin to explore the new world that is based on playing with language. Sally Goddard Blythe (2011) reminds everyone who works in early years settings that rhymes introduce babies and young children not just to their particular cultural heritage but to the accents embedded in that language:

> In the early years music is the pre-verbal expression of language and prepares the ear, voice and brain for speech.
>
> (Goddard Blythe, 2011, p. 38)

Storytellers seem to understand this innate rhythmic pattern within language and have become skilled at using different kinds of intonation when they chant, sing or tell stories and rhymes. We know that young listeners readily respond to language that is patterned, fluent and pleasing to the ear. Children are active participants in the creation of this culture and, given the opportunity, will create their own chants as they begin to interpret a rhyme or a story. And there is plenty of evidence too that shows how this awareness of the rhythm of spoken text supports young children's early reading development (Minns, 1997, p. 107).

You are ideally positioned to encourage babies and young children to enjoy music and musical tones, by making playful sounds with your mouths for them to imitate or singing songs to children as you go through daily routines with them. In doing so, you will become a traditional storyteller yourself, creating sounds and conveying atmosphere and interest to your chants and stories. The repetition of these "playful sounds" helps young children to develop phonological awareness because they learn to distinguish different tones and listen for even the smallest changes in the use of vowels or consonants, a skill that will be needed when children learn to read and they begin to make the link between sounds and the letters of the alphabet.

Indeed, where appropriate, we have suggested activities in Part II of this book that concentrate on the teaching of phonics in ways that are pleasurable. Rhymes and stories are particularly valuable for putting the teaching of phonics in context. They often use alliteration, where the same initial sound is repeated over and over again, and they delight in the playful use of patterned language where the beginnings and endings of words and phrases have the characteristics of a rhyme. Goddard Blythe's (2011) observations of young children have convinced her that nursery rhymes are key to helping young children develop this auditory discrimination because they "mimic the rise and falling patterns of a complicated, compound rhythmic language" (p. 51). These patterns make chants and stories memorable for young listeners.

Laying the foundations for literary appreciation

Paley proposed, while working with very young children, that:

> We cannot...do without adult storytelling. The poetry and prose of the best children's books enter our minds when we are young and sing back to us all our lives.
>
> (Paley, 1990, p. 44)

This early love of language takes children into imaginary worlds and gives them scope for entering the world of a story between the covers of a book, exploring events and talking about what might happen next, just as they do when they listen to an oral story or rhyme. In Cathy Nutbrown's (2011) terms, stories are a source of "nourishment for the minds of young children" (p. 128). They ignite their current interests and feed into their meaning making processes. Children gain new ideas and learn about patterns of behaviour in stories and apply these to their play.

At the end of each of the ten practical chapters in Part II of this book, we suggest that you might want to share a published book that makes links with the main theme. We have chosen these books with care: each has literary merit and is beautifully written, the subject matter is interesting, the language is delightful and playful and the book can be read and re-read many times. Significantly, the illustrations complement the text and give opportunities for discussion.

Children as creators of new rhymes and stories

The manner in which we share rhymes and stories, including our choice of words and phrases, can help children to re-create images in their heads and provide them with mental pictures of what is happening. Your ideas and your choice of language when you recite rhymes and tell stories in your own words combine with the children's imagination and work in tandem to generate meaning and help children to create pictures in their heads as they explore their own invented worlds. Rhymes like *I had a little marigold seed* and stories like *The Enormous Turnip* and *The Elves and the Shoemaker* are rich in meaning. They grip a child's imagination because they invite children to enter new worlds and help them to create mental images of the characters and to think about how events will unfold. These images stay in children's minds when they revisit the world of the story. Many children's picture books are richly illustrated by talented artists, but there are times when children need the opportunity to make their own pictures in their minds and create their own scenes. This ability helps them to feel their own imaginings are just as significant as those represented in published artwork. Betty Rosen would agree. With years of storytelling experience behind her, she has observed that: "pictures in the imagination of the receiver of a told story have more impact than pictures in a storybook" (1991, p. 20). And as children translate words and phrases into mental images, they are learning how to make meaning. This is a creative intellectual activity. Hugh Lupton (2001), a professional storyteller, maintains that "storytelling is a language of pictures" (p. 10). He advises those of us who tell oral stories to take "the kind of pace that allows people to visualise things as you go. You want to leave room for them to see things for themselves" (Lupton, 2001, p. 22).

We have discussed the theoretical positions of Vygotsky and Bruner, showing that all development and learning happen within social contexts, so it is important that early literacy initiatives are mutually enjoyable. As children participate in rhymes and storytelling with you, their attentive teacher or with family members, they contribute by joining in, inventing new characters and events and, perhaps most significantly, entering the world of make-believe as they tell their own stories. Children who are encouraged to respond to stories and rhymes by re-telling their own personal stories are at a real advantage. Comments like "I planted a seed with my mummy" or "My shoes went to be mended" show that they are beginning to make sense of things that have happened to them and relate these to the world of The Elves and the Shoemaker or The Enormous Turnip.

When children tell their own stories, they are developing a sense of self and an identity as storytellers in their own right. At the same time, they understand that their stories are valued by their teacher and by the other children in their group. So, questions like "Has anything like this happened to you?" and "Do you know anyone like this?" will often kick-start a thoughtful discussion where children take the lead and begin to ask their own questions – and sometimes these questions are enormously challenging, such as: "How come the gingerbread man was real when he was made out of playdough?" or "Why did the gingerbread man trust the fox?"

These questions were generated by a six-year-old who had just listened to The Gingerbread Man, and they are an indication that young children develop sophisticated thought processes and cognitive understanding when they listen to stories. At the same time, they show how it is possible for young children to develop empathy as they engage with the thoughts of the characters in a story, feeling compassion for them and developing insights into their own behaviour. Stories are woven in and out of children's lives to help them make connections, see things in different ways, stand in other people's shoes, imagine other possibilities and reveal significant emotional states.

Sometimes children re-invent themselves as the central character in a well-known story; at other times, they weave their real-life experience into a story they have invented. And thus they shape their life through narrative. Here, for example, is part of a story that Jacob told his teacher as he recalled his visit to Kenya to see his family who lived in a local village. Note how he incorporates elements from fairy stories he knows (the hen and the fox, the repeated phrase) into his original narrative and see how his knowledge of story language influences his own use of words and phrases as he builds up a picture of his own world and organises his thoughts into a narrative account:

> In Kenya there used to be this sort of forest but my mum told me not to go in the forest because there used to be snakes and monkeys and spiders. Once, I was bored and I didn't have nothing to do so I held my hen and I said, "Do you want to go in the forest?" and my hen went "Cock-a-doodle-do", so I thought it said "yes", so I took him to the forest and there was a fox there and it kept on going like this: "Arrh, Arrh", and my hen kept on going "Cock-a-doodle-do", and then I got scared and I shouted and I screamed and screamed and screamed and then my uncle came and he said, "What's wrong?" And I said that I think there was a fox or something, but then he told me that it was a dog and it wouldn't do anything.

Jacob's experience has become part of his storytelling world. He has created this extended monologue to help him to weave the emotions and events of his experience into a narrative and told his story with energy and gusto. Fortunately for him, his teacher appreciates children's own stories and understands that personal narratives like Jacob's have a huge role to play in children's understanding of themselves and in their wider learning that goes far beyond their value as entertainment at the end of the school day. Jacob is working hard to reconstruct this series of events, which obviously frightened him, and perhaps he retold other versions of this story to family members and friends. David Booth and Bob Barton (2000) would certainly value Jacob's story and give credit to his teacher for encouraging him to record it. "We must value the family stories," they write, for "they are spun gold into story and they add to our wealth as storyers" (p. 29).

The importance of play

Children play with stories and weave them into their own lives as they make meaning. Sometimes props can support such play, but there is no need to search out for a hen or fox to support Jacob's play, for example. Any object will do. Indeed, as Tina Bruce (2017) advocates in her updated interpretation of the work of Friedrich Froebel (1782–1853), "the less literal the toys provided the more the imagination works" (p. 14). Children are able to transform anything, for example, a wooden bricks or a large leaf, into what they need. Your regular use of mime to illustrate rhymes and stories will encourage them to do the same.

Provide opportunities for children and support them to re-enact stories with objects or symbols. As Bruce and Dyke (2017) remind us, symbols stand for something else and therefore encourage creative play.

> As soon as children begin to use symbols they are moving from the present, literal, concrete and real to something that is not necessarily present or real. They can think in more abstract and imaginative ways. They are no longer tied to the present.
>
> (Bruce and Dyke, 2017)

Set up small world areas outdoors and indoors and support children to develop stories using anything as props or by performing actions. The best play takes place when you play with children. Children might reference one of the characters from a rhyme or story you shared and so imagine themselves in other worlds, beyond their present reality. These playful opportunities using small world symbols or bodily actions are of immense value. As Bruce and Dyke (2017) propose:

> Play [...] helps children to co-ordinate their ideas and feelings and make sense of their relationships with family, friends and culture. It promotes flexible, adaptive, imaginative, innovative behaviour and makes children into whole people, able to keep balancing their lives in a fast-changing world.
>
> (Bruce and Dyke, 2017)

Thus, play helps children to make sense of situations and, in Piagetian terms, accommodate new ideas and experiences. Play is an anchor for children. We suggest that it is your role to facilitate play and support it. The stories and rhymes you share can trigger new ideas for rich play.

Bruce suggests that the best learning takes place when both adults and children contribute to and participate in the play together. When both are active and fully immersed in the play, "the children wallow in it" (Bruce, 2017, p. 11). When the play ends, it ends. It cannot be bottled or preserved. As Bruce writes:

> Play is a process. It has no products. When the play episode ends or fades, it vanishes as quickly as it arrived. Unlike a formal dance or song, written story, painting or constructed model, it cannot be set into a static, concrete result or finalised form. This is a great strength of play. It cannot be pinned down. It flows, and has all the hallmarks of improvisation.
>
> (Bruce, 2017, p. 14)

And so, teach children catchy rhymes and traditional stories and allow them to re-create them in their own way for as long or as little as they like. Take an interest and participate in their creations, helping them to deepen and extend their play. Your loving attention and sensitive intervention will establish the conditions whereby children create their own rhymes and tell their own stories as they "wallow" (Bruce, 2017, p. 14) in their play.

Rhymes and stories to encourage discussion

When a child says "The naughty crocodile shouldn't have done that," we recognise that this child is developing the capacity to listen carefully to what is happening in a story and to make intelligent judgements about the actions of certain characters. This kind of interaction will only happen if you encourage thoughtful discussions and give children the opportunity to explore ideas in rhymes and stories. Students in our early years course discovered that they could foster this kind of valuable relationship with children in four particular ways: asking challenging questions and inviting the children to ask their own questions, encouraging children to take the lead, focusing on particular words that are of interest to the children and, finally, supplying additional information that relates to the subject matter in the rhymes and stories.

Challenging questions help children to think critically; so, when you tell the story of The North Wind and the Sun, rather than ask "What colour was Mr. Jones' cloak?", ask instead "How do you think Mr. Jones was feeling when the wind blew?"

Many young children enjoy re-telling their own versions of stories into a dictaphone. Six-year-old Sue and Vicki and five-year-old Ian told their own version of The Three Little Pigs. Here is a small part of their re-telling, which lasted for about 20 minutes:

Vicki: *My turn. The last little pig met a man with some bricks. He asked him if he could have some bricks and he gave him the bricks. He built his house and it took him a very long time and the wolf came along.*

Ian: *And he knocked on the door and he said, Little Pig, Little Pig, let me come in. I am hungry and poor.*

Sue: *No, no. By the hair of my chinny chin chin, I will not let you come in. Then I'll huff and I'll puff and I'll blow your house in said the wolf.*

It is worth noting that these children have internalised some of the literary language of this story as well as some of the more archaic phrases associated with the text. They are also learning to turn-take and to listen carefully to each other. Every now and again, it is possible to hear "planning whispers" on the recording, as the children talk together to prepare the next part of the story. This planning talk is important: the children are learning the social skills of turn-taking and listening to each other's ideas as they pool ideas and negotiate the task of re-telling the story. The dictaphone allowed their teacher to listen later on and to discover how much these children were achieving.

Carol Fox (1983) studied the early narrative stories of a five-year-old called Jill. She became what Fox calls the "broadcaster-storyteller" (p. 17) of stories she invented. Jill experimented with a range of sound effects and different voices as she took on the roles of both broadcaster and storyteller. Jill shows us that we should never underestimate a young child's ability to enter the world of the imagination. If children are given the opportunity they will re-create, explore and hold on to scenarios of their own making. We hope that the rhymes and stories in this book will act as a springboard for children's imaginative re-tellings in your own nurseries and classrooms.

Rhymes and stories to develop the imagination

You will notice that among the suggested activities in Part II of this book, we include the headings such as drawing and painting and role play. Put simply, this activity is an invitation to the children you work with to use their love of image-making to enrich their understanding of the events and characters they have met in the rhymes and stories you share with them and to translate the pictures in their heads into drawing, paint and colour. This activity allows them to inspect the events of a story through the images they make on paper. There is much more to this creative process than we usually have time to notice in the busy world of the nursery or classroom. Elizabeth Coates and Andrew Coates (2021) have shown through their close observations of two six-year-olds that when children draw images and talk about them, they enhance not only their developing artistic skills but their use of language too and their ability to solve difficult problems. Crucially, Coates and Coates argue that

...drawing and talking together allows children to become aware of and thereby to recognise the potential of each other's images for their own thinking, leading to a situation in which a more profound sharing of thoughts and ideas is possible.

(Coates and Coates, 2021, p. 2)

In doing so, they continue, the children they observed "developed the capability to solve problems by making potent visual images" (p. 12) and "achieved intellectual nourishment" (p. 11) from their artistic discussions. And so, we suggest that it is important to give children opportunities to re-present stories in different ways and talk to you and to each other about their creations because this enriches their cognitive abilities at the same time as supporting their artistic development.

Rhymes and stories to support mathematical development

Caroline McGrath's (2014) research has shown that stories often contain problems that lend themselves to mathematical discussion. Her work with young children has foregrounded the ways that creative storytelling and storymaking, and in particular the use of props and puppets, can support mathematical development and problem-solving in the early years and help to make "abstract mathematical ideas visual for children" (2014, p. 140). We have argued that one of your key roles as an early years teacher is to invite children to express their responses to the stories and rhymes you share with them. One way of doing this is to explore these connections with mathematical patterns. The use of numbers features in many of the stories and rhymes in this book. For example, Four little pussy cats came to my door and Five little peas in a pea-pod pressed will help children to consolidate their understanding of number and the ordering of events. Relative size – small, bigger, biggest – is a feature of story language too. In the story of the Three Billy Goats Gruff, "The first one … was the smallest; the second one … was a bit bigger; the third one … was the biggest of all." These examples, and others in Part II, present opportunities to discuss these aspects of number. Seeing the threeness of three, touching three objects or taking three steps can help children build their knowledge and understanding of number.

Chapter conclusion

In this chapter, we have argued that sharing rhymes and stories helps to create a powerful bond between you and the children you teach and that by listening to forms of patterned language children become sensitive to the literary styles and rhymes that form the basis of many rhymes and stories from the folk tradition. With your encouragement, children begin to join in with these rhymes and chants, to create their own re-tellings and to share their personal stories. The concluding chapter in Part I of this book offers a range of practical ideas for learning and sharing rhymes and stories and for encouraging response.

References

Booth, D. & Barton, B. (2000), Story Works: How Teachers Can Use Shared Stories in the New Curriculum, Markham Ontario: Pembroke.

Bruce, T. (2017), Ponderings on play: Froebelian assemblages. In: Bruce, T., Hakkarainen, P., & Bredikyte, M. eds., *The Routledge International Handbook of Early Childhood Play*, 1st edn., Routledge. https://0-doi-org.pugwash.lib.warwick.ac.uk/10.4324/9781315735290 [10 February 2023].

Bruce, T. & Dyke, J. (2017), EYFS best practice – Learning from Froebel … the symbolic life of the child. *Nursery World*, 17 April 2017.

Bruner, J. (1976), *Actual Minds, Possible Worlds*, Cambridge, Mass, and London: Harvard University Press.

Center of the Developing Child, Harvard University, *How-to: 5 Steps for Brain-Building Serve and Return*. https://developingchild.harvard.edu/resources/5-steps-for-brain-building-serve-and-return/

Coates, E. & Coates, A. (2021), Images in Words and Pictures: Issues Arising from a Shared Experience of Talking and Drawing. *Children and Society*, 35(2), pp. 244–258.

Conkbayir, M. (2016), Why You Can't Phone in Human Interaction, *The Times Educational Supplement*, 5229. https://www.tes.com/magazine/archived/why-you-cant-phone-human-interaction

Crystal, D. (1987), *The Cambridge Encyclopaedia of Language*, Cambridge: Cambridge University Press.

Fox, C. (1983), *At the Very Edge of the Forest: The Influence of Literature on Storytelling* by Children, London: Cassell.

Goddard Blythe, S. (2011), *The Genius of Natural Childhood: Secrets of Thriving Children*, Stroud: Hawthorn Press.

Lupton, H. (2001) *The Dreaming of Place: Storytelling and Landscape*. Reading: Society for Storytelling Press.

Malloch, S. & Trevarthen, C. (2018), 'The Human Nature of Music', *Frontiers in Psychology*, 9. doi: 10.3389/fpsyg.2018.01680. [20 February 2021].

McGrath, C. (2014), *Teaching Mathematics Through Story: A Creative Approach for the Early Years*, London and New York: Routledge.

Meek, M. (1988), *How Texts Teach What Readers Learn*, South Woodchester, Stroud: The Thimble Press.

Minns, H. (1997), *Read It to Me Now! Learning at Home and at School*. Buckingham: Open University Press.

Niland, A. (2015), "Row, Row, Row Your Boat": Singing, Identity and Belonging in a Nursery, *International Journal of Early Years Education*, 23(1), pp. 4–16.

Nutbrown, C. (2011), *Threads of Thinking: Schemas and Young Children's Learning*. 4th edn, London: Sage.

Paley, V.G. (1990), *The Boy Who Would Be a Helicopter: The Uses of Storytelling in the Classroom*, Cambridge, Mass., and London: Harvard University Press.

Rosen, B. (1991), "Is My Story Too Frightening?" In: Shapers and Polishers: Teachers as Storytellers, London: Mary Glasgow.

Scholes, P. (1970) *The Oxford Companion to Music*. 10th edn. Oxford: Oxford University Press.

Trevarthen, C. (2013), 'What Young Children Know About Living and Learning With Companions', *Nordisk Barnehageforskning*, 6. doi: 10.7577/nbf.441.

Trevarthen, C. (2015), Communicative Musicality or Stories of Truth and Beauty in the Sound of Moving, Sémiotique de la musique, Dossier 3. *Music, Song, Language* 165–194. doi: 10.4000/signata.1075.

Vygotsky, L. (1978), *Mind in Society: The Development of Higher Psychological Processes*, Cambridge, Mass: Harvard University Press.

Wells, G. (1986), *The Meaning Makers: Children Learning Language and Using Language to Learn.* Portsmouth: Heinemann Educational Books.

Wood, D., Bruner, J., & Ross, G. (1976), The Role of Tutoring in Problem Solving. *Journal of Child Psychology and Psychiatry*, 17(2), pp. 89–100.

3 The art of reciting rhymes and telling stories

The Reading Framework in England (DfE, 2021) proposes that "even small children who have difficulty focusing in class will sit with rapt attention in the presence of a good storyteller" (p. 29). The Early Years Foundation Stage in England (DfE, 2021) highlights the importance of storytelling to promote communication and states that this is best supported:

> Through conversation, storytelling and role-play, where children share their ideas with support and modeling from their teacher, and sensitive questioning that invites them to elaborate...
>
> (DfE, 2021, p. 8)

In the first two chapters of Part I of this book, we discussed the reasons why rhymes and stories are crucial for young children's social, cultural, emotional and intellectual development. This concluding chapter of Part I concentrates on the art of oral storytelling and the reciting of rhymes, and in particular, it looks at the practicalities – that is to say, ways of choosing, learning, telling and sharing rhymes and stories while at the same time encouraging children to respond creatively in a warm, supportive environment. Everybody who works with babies and early years children spends time sharing picturebooks and rhyming texts with them; indeed, early years settings provide a wealth of beautiful picture books which are often dipped into by staff, families and children alike. The cover picture, the illustrations, the language and the written text combine to enrich your story sessions, and we urge you to continue sharing these books with children to help them to develop their love of literacy and to give them a lifelong desire to read.

But this chapter aims to take this process further, by suggesting various ways in which you can develop your ability to *recite rhymes by heart* and *acquire the art of storytelling without using a book as a prop*. Very few of us are professional storytellers or entertainers. Even so, we are all capable of conveying the magic of rhymes and stories

DOI: 10.4324/9781003358633-4

to young listeners. The writer Doris Lessing (2007) reminds us that "the storyteller is deep inside every one of us. The story-maker is always with us." We agree with her. You don't need to be a performer or an actor; just be yourself. Enjoy the rhymes and stories, and the rest will follow, as you become a reciter and creator of rhymes and a teller and inventor of stories.

If you are new to this way of sharing rhymes and stories, you might want to begin by choosing one particular chapter in Part II simply because you like the rhymes and are drawn to a certain stories or because you believe the children in your setting would benefit from some of the suggested activities. And so, we hope that you will use a particular chapter to stimulate your teaching. Thereafter, we hope that you will plan rhyming and story sessions in response to the children's interests or to reflect a generic theme your school or nursery might be focusing on. Each chapter suggests links to overarching themes, such as friendship or caring for the environment. You are likely therefore to become a rhyme and story collector yourself, attentive to the texts, sounds and patterns that you can use and adapt to build your literary bank, just as Sarah did when she was an early years teacher (see Chapter 1). The rhymes, stories and activities in Part II are designed for your own enjoyment as much as for the children's. Whatever choices and decisions you make, we hope that you will strive to make each session enjoyable for all involved, including your-selves, because if you love a particular rhyme or story, your delight will be reflected in the children's responses and you can enter a magical space together.

We want to encourage you to learn the rhymes and stories in Part II and to adapt them to suit the particular tastes of your children, using your voice and eyes to create suspense, to introduce pauses and to be inventive with your use of props. The collection in Part II is designed to act as a springboard for your own creativity and serve as the beginning of your personal collection of rhymes and stories.

There are two important reasons why we believe you should consider sharing rhymes and stories orally, face-to-face, rather than reading them aloud. We have already talked about the way that storytellers form a bond with their young listeners. One important way of interacting is by making eye contact with them. You can do this to a much greater extent without a book because you can gaze directly at the children and they can see your face and eyes and watch your changing expressions. If you're not holding a book you can use your hands and arms to make gestures, such as screwing your fingers up tight to make a little mouse face, or showing the mouse scampering away by using the fingers of one hand to run up the other arm. And of course your hands are free to show the children props or to introduce a puppet. Include wider families in your storytelling so that all can learn from this approach and build on the stories and rhymes in different contexts. These features will make the story come alive as you transform it and retell it in your own words. This requires an act of imagination on your part as you visualise the narrative for yourself and engage with the world of feeling inside the story. In doing so, you will reflect the style and expression and also the shape and pattern of the story but at the same time make it uniquely your own.

Secondly, without a book, you are free to adapt, modify and re-shape the stories and find exactly the right words and phrases to meet the needs of your young listeners in order to convey the meaning and the emotions. Sometimes there will be great tension, and your voice will sound dramatic, vivid and exciting, as in this rhyme:

> Your teeth are ferocious,
> You think you're the boss,
> But you'll never stop me
> From swimming across!
>   (Crocodiles and Monkeys)

At other times, the words of a story will offer comfort and consolation, and your voice and facial expressions will reflect this:

> There was plenty of food for everyone, and the people were always kind to each other. From then on, they all thanked God for the good things of the earth, and were never hungry again.
> (See Precious Toys and Playthings)

As you try out this approach on different occasions, you will gain the confidence to be creative with the written text. It is likely that one of the children will comment on something that has happened in a rhyme or story, and you are then free to explore this, perhaps adding an extra event and inventing new possibilities and variations. In practical terms, you might find you have less time, or more time, than you thought in which to deliver your rhyme or story, and you can shorten or lengthen it to fit into the time slot available.

You will inevitably need to adapt the examples provided in this book, especially if you support new arrivals such as refugees or children from migrant families. These children may have suffered loss and trauma and be unable to concentrate for longer periods, particularly if you are telling a story in English. In such cases, we advise you to be prepared to improvise, for example with props to aid understanding, and allow children to change the course of the session. A familiar tale may remind them of a similar one from their own culture, so encourage children and their families to tell the stories they know or repeat the stories you share in their own words.

Choosing rhymes and stories

In Part II, you will find a rich mixture of rhymes, traditional stories, stories from the European tradition and stories from other cultures to choose from and add to your repertoire. We have chosen them because we believe they will extend young children's imaginative experience and their knowledge of how written language is used in literary forms in the rhymes and stories. In the first instance, we encourage you to look through Part II of this book and choose a rhyme or story that you love and that feels right for you and the children you support. Each child's experience of rhymes and stories will be different; some will already know and love nursery rhymes and tales; other children will have not met them before and will find listening to them very difficult. Some children will have very little knowledge of English and will struggle at first to make sense of the words and phrases. And so, your choice of rhymes and stories might be a new experience for you and for the children; nevertheless, we encourage you to be brave and to challenge the children so that you extend their language and their experience of the world, always having a respect for their development and their increasing maturity. You might want to choose a particular story that you feel you can learn so that you become confident and familiar with the events and the words and can put the book to one side. Children love the stories that are loved by the people who tell them, and they love to hear stories retold again and again, anticipating the pleasure they bring. Their appreciation and delight will mirror your own pleasure in sharing them, so don't be afraid to ask "Which story shall we have today?" so that they learn to make their own choices. There will be times when you want to introduce a brand new rhyme or story. This is important too because it offers new challenges and gives you an opportunity to have conversations that help the children to see new possibilities, discuss unusual vocabulary, talk about different characters and think about reaching out into a series of events that are new to them so you catch their imagination, present opportunities for them to enrich their language and help them to shape their ideas.

Setting up an area for rhymes and stories

You can't always choose where you and the children will sit for your rhyme and story sessions, but if you can, choose a quiet and comfortable area with no distractions. The way you organise this area has a bearing on what the children expect when you all go and sit there. If you make the area beautiful, it shows the children that you value it, and they will respond accordingly. Cushions, rugs or blankets, soft chairs and beanbags can all be used to make the area cosy, so everybody feels comfortable and relaxed. This is particularly important for children who are not able to experience this kind of warm and welcoming environment at home. Sharing rhymes and stories in these unhurried and pleasurable conditions supports children's social and emotional development. Think about where you are going to sit so that you can keep close eye contact with the children and have room to show them props and pictures if these form part of your session. Some children may want to snuggle up to you to begin with and move to face you when they feel more confident. Some teachers have a particularly comfortable chair that they reserve for these sessions. You might choose to sit cross-legged with the children on the carpet or to sit on a chair above the children; either way, make sure they can see your facial expressions.

Sometimes the children will respond to you with complete silence and stillness as they think about your words, but small children often like to move their bodies, so try to ensure that they have room to join in with the actions of a rhyme or story, using their fingers for counting, their hands for clapping and their feet for stamping in time with the rhythm. It is important that you have room to move around too, so choose a chair or a position on the floor that gives you the space to move your arms around and to show a variety of props. Your comfort is as important as the children's.

Finding the right time to share a rhyme or story

Loris Malaguzzi, the pedagogist, psychologist and thinker behind the Reggio Emilia approach, proposed that creativity emerges from daily experiences (Edwards et al, 2014) and the timing of your daily experience of sharing rhymes and stories is something you might want to consider. Of course, you will apply your experience and professionalism in choosing the right time. It is possible that, on some days, you may choose *not* to gather children for rhymes and stories but simply to weave in spontaneous rhyming and storying as part of children's sustained play. It is not always appropriate to follow your plan for the day. As Nutbrown (2011) articulated so well,

> ...*adult-constructed* continuity is not necessarily the kind of continuity that fulfills children's need for continuity in their own personal learning and thinking, and adult-constructed continuity which is informed only by external constructions of continuity is unlikely to contain the responsible opportunities for learning and thinking to which many young children readily respond.
>
> (p. 44)

Thus, interrupting children's rich and purposeful play to share rhymes and stories may be unfruitful, or imposing a content-based theme for too long may inhibit children's creativity.

Nevertheless, on most days, it is likely that you will find an appropriate time to recite rhymes and tell stories. In the home context, find a comfortable part of the room and choose a quiet, unrushed moment to share a rhyme or story. It is often a good idea to do this after a meal when children are not hungry. Parents often read to their children after bath time when they are ready for bed and feel comfortable, warm and safe in an atmosphere of love and trust. At first, you might want to choose familiar stories and rhymes, so the children feel at ease and delight in telling you over and over again what the characters are like and what is going to happen next. Introduce new rhymes and stories gradually.

In the classroom or nursery setting, you will know when the best time is for sharing a rhyme or story with the children you work with. This could be a spontaneous session in response to children's requests for their favourite story, or it might be to help them cope with a particular emotion. Many early years settings have a special timetabled slot for story sessions, sometimes at the beginning of the day, just before or after lunch or at the end of a session. Children get used to this routine and look forward to it, and having a particular timetabled slot certainly helps you to plan ahead, especially if you are intending to introduce any of the follow-up activities when you will definitely need to allow sufficient time for the children to respond.

The end of the school or nursery day is a good time for you to gather the children together. It is a good opportunity to invite parents, carers and other family members to come and listen too. But there are other times during the day when children are not so tired and a rhyme or story can lead to greater involvement with follow-up activities, so try to vary the times when you recite rhymes and tell stories. Be spontaneous, and seize opportunities for children to enjoy rhymes and stories at different times of the day. Whatever time you choose, we believe that rhymes and stories should be an integral part of your school day.

Ways of learning stories

Some people feel daunted at the thought of having to learn to tell a story, but there is really no need to try and memorise each sentence. Instead, use your own words to retell the story in your own words so that it sounds spontaneous and fresh, though of course you might want to memorise some of the well-known refrains that recur throughout, such as *Who's that trip-trapping over my bridge?*. When you use your own words, the story will feel fresh and have the quality of being told for the first time, even though you might have told it over and over again.

It is a good idea to experiment with different ways of learning a story until you find the one that is right for you. Over time, you will acquire your own technique as you reflect on your own storytelling style and respond sensitively to the children. It does not matter if you lose your way. Children are very receptive, and they will engage with the ideas and still find themselves transported to another world.

The students who took part in our Stories and Storytelling module as part of their Early Childhood Degree course spent a great deal of time discussing ways of learning a story, and below are eight of their suggestions that you might like to try for yourselves.

■ *Read the story over and over again so that it gets fixed in your head and you become familiar with the events and the characters.*

■ *Write the story down word for word so that you understand the structure.*

■ *Jot down a summary of the story, or jot down the key words, so that you remember the main points.*

■ *Divide the story into chunks. Write just the first two lines in your own words and commit these to memory, then go on to read, write and remember the next chunk.*

■ *Go through the actions in your head. This will help you to understand what the characters are doing.*

■ *Build pictures in your head of what's happening so that you create a mental map or storyboard. This process of visualisation will help you to recall the sequence of events in the story.*

■ *Use the five senses. Try to get a clear picture in your own mind of things in the story that you can see, hear, taste, smell and touch. Describing these will help the children to use their own sensory awareness. For example, "The turnip soup smelled delicious and it tasted even better. It was thick and sweet and juicy"; "Baby bear's porridge was creamy and sweet and Goldilocks could taste the sugar that Mother Bear had sprinkled on top."*

■ *Say the story aloud to yourself when you're on your own in the car or when you're relaxing in the bath. Remember, practice makes perfect!*

Ways of reciting rhymes

The Early Years Foundation Stage in England (DfE, 2021) highlights the ways in which rhymes and poems can support children's learning and development across all areas. For example, the document states that:

■ "Engaging [children] actively in stories, non-fiction, rhymes and poems … will give [them] the opportunity to thrive" (p. 8);

■ children are helped to become literate when adults "enjoy rhymes, poems and songs together" (p. 9); and

■ "listening to a broad selection of stories, non-fiction, rhymes and poems will foster [children's] understanding of our culturally, socially, technologically and ecologically diverse world" (p. 10).

Some of the above suggestions for learning a story and getting it ready for telling will also be applicable to learning rhymes, but there are some crucial differences. In particular, *the words of the rhyme cannot change* because the rhythm has to be regular and the rhyming words at the end of each line have been chosen with care. So, for example:

> Miss Polly had a dolly who was sick, sick, sick,
> So she called for the doctor to be quick, quick, quick
> The doctor came with his bag and his hat
> And he knocked on the door with a rat-a-tat-tat.
> (See Precious Toys and Playthings)

You can sometimes change names or nouns in a rhyme to make them more referable to your children, for example:

Natasha had a dolly who was sick, sick, sick

If you do, you will need to take care to keep the rhythm and rhyme as known in written or oral traditions. This is what makes them catchy and timeless.

So, how do you go about learning a rhyme like this? Probably the best way is to keep saying it to yourself over and over again, taking advantage of the repetition and the rhyming words that will help you to predict the ending of each line.

It is important to choose rhymes that you enjoy so that children can catch your enthusiasm. Create opportunities in daily and weekly routines to recite little rhymes to match children's actions. For example, you might want to sing *Sunday, Monday, Tuesday, Wednesday, Thursday, Friday, Saturday too* or other "days of the week" songs as you talk about the weather or match the weather icons to different days of the week. Or, you could make up words to the tune of *Here we go round the mulberry bush* as you help children to prepare the table for lunch.

This is the way we wash our hands
Wash our hands
Wash our hands
This is the way we wash our hands
Before we eat our lunch.

This is the way we lay the table
Lay the table
Lay the table
This is the way we lay the table
Before we eat our lunch.

This is the way we pour the water
Pour the water
Pour the water
This is the way we pour the water
Before we eat our lunch.

Etc…

Ways of telling stories

In the ensuing three sections, the focus is on you, the rhymer and storyteller. It offers suggestions for beginning and ending your sessions, using your voice and facial expressions and gestures and introducing props and puppets. You will probably already be very good at reading aloud to children, but the experience of reciting a rhyme or telling a story without the book might be new to you. There is another thing to consider too; the children in your setting might never have listened to rhymes and stories shared orally, without a book, and the following ideas will introduce them to new ways of listening and sharing and add to their experience of enjoying the rhythm and shape of written language and enlarge their interest in stories.

Beginning and ending your session

Once the children are settled, you can develop a ritual for beginning your session. Perhaps you can go and sit in your favourite story chair, or you might get the children's attention by singing or chanting a particular phrase that you repeat over and over again, clapping as you do so, cupping your ears to show that it's time to listen and putting your finger to your lips as you say "Sssh." Here are a few suggestions:

It's time! It's time!
Come and listen to my rhyme!

Let's all listen to my story!
Here we go! Let's begin...

It's time for a story!
Are you ready? Are you ready?
Sssh! It's time! It's time.

It's time to tell a story
It's time to tell a story
Are you listening?
Are you listening?
Are you listening?

The first sentence of your story is important for establishing the context and introducing the characters and for helping to establish the bond between teller and told. Here are a few conventional beginnings for you to work with:

When I was a very little, my grandma told me this story and now I want to share it with you...
Once, in a deep dark forest, there lived a family of bears...
Once upon a time there was a farmyard. Mother Hen lived in the farmyard with her chicks...
Long ago in the time of mystery there lived a strange little man...

Story beginnings like these are an important way of helping the children to immerse themselves in the world of their imagination, as they listen to the musicality of the story language and begin to ease themselves away from the walls of their classroom or nursery into an unfamiliar world of magical characters, talking animals, strange events and unusual words and phrases.

Endings are important too. In Chapter 2, we discussed the importance of leaving young listeners with hope at the end of a story or rhyme, no matter how dark the content. The final sentence therefore is very important. Here are some ideas:

And this is the story my grandma told me many years ago…
And they all lived happily ever after…
A story from India, many thousands of years ago…
And where he went, nobody knows…but one thing is for sure, he never came back to bother them again…

Using your voice

We hope you will experiment with using your voice in different ways to convey the mood of the rhyme or story. You could use different voices or accents to match the size or age of each character, such as Little Red Hen's assertive and rather resigned decision: "*Very well. I'll have to do it all by myself!*" (see Growing Things). Children will become conscious of the way your voice rises and falls in pitch and volume to indicate drama, excitement or stillness, and they will listen carefully as your voice becomes louder or softer, faster or slower, to express a particular feeling or mood and to signal the climax. This subtle use of your voice will help young children to understand how to use their own voice to tell a story or recite a rhyme effectively.

Using props and puppets

Despite this suggestion, there is actually no need to use props, pictures or puppets to help you to tell your story – your eyes, voice, hand and facial gestures will convey meaning on their own, so don't feel you have to introduce props just for their own sake. However, from time to time, artefacts can stimulate discussion and lead children gently into the main theme, helping children to make the transition from the world of the classroom into the imaginary world of the story. So, you might develop one or two puppets to enact different teaching points. In maths, for example, one might give or take playthings from the other in a friendly and enjoyable way to support children's understanding of "one more" and "one less." Similarly, you might show the children a particular shoe since this can spark discussion about shoes and lead into the rhyme and story in Boots and Shoes. If you are telling the story of The Little Red Hen (See Baking Bread), it is possible that the children will never have seen wheat, so try to show them what it looks like, either in a picture or by having some wheat for them to examine. If you are telling The Flying Turtle (See Water for Life) from India, you could use a picture of a turtle and talk about what it looks like – its mouth, legs and feet and its shell, for example. If you have been lucky enough to see a turtle yourself, in an aquarium or on a tropical beach, tell the children about your experience. They will enjoy listening as you share your own personal story.

Simple musical instruments can emphasise the sense of rhythm in a rhyme or chant. Ask the children to clap to the rhythm or make particular sounds with their fingers or feet. You could use simple or homemade percussion instruments to echo particular sounds in the rhymes – *"A-rap-a-tap-a-rap-a-tap"* (see Boots and Shoes) – or use a rainstick to make the sound of rain falling. You don't need expensive instruments. Tear some newspaper or crumple it to make interesting sounds. Make simple shakers with empty, clean yogurt pots. Tap your feet.

As we suggested earlier with reference to the experience of Afghan children (p. 9), it is important to set rhymes and stories in a wider context. For example, by encouraging new refugee children to handle objects and go down their own tangents, according to their interests, Sarah brought in a wooden shoe mould and mimed covering the shoe mould with leather to show the outline of the beautiful shoe in the rhyme and to give the children an idea of how it was made. She also pointed to children's feet as she recited "Cobbler, cobbler, mend my shoe" (see Boots and Shoes). One of the children showed recognition of what the topic was about. This child took the shoe mould and mimed the actions herself. Activities like this can help children who are learning English to extend their imaginative experience and broaden their knowledge of how language is used in stories. In this way, rhymes and stories can build on their own language experience and give them personal encouragement.

Encouraging response

In each chapter of Part II, we have made a great many suggestions for follow-up activities to use with babies and older children. We have designed these activities to reflect and illuminate the potential of the rhymes and the story in each chapter, and we hope that you will dip into these activities as part of your rhyme and storytelling sessions. These activities include children re-telling or acting out the rhymes and stories and writing their own versions, sharing their own personal stories and discussing and enacting important elements of the plot as they take on the role of a variety of characters. Indeed, the Reading Framework in England (2021) emphasises the importance of role play because it helps children to "reflect on how a character might think, feel and behave at key moments, and explore motives and intentions" (p. 31).

We have included a range of ideas to support early literacy and mathematical and scientific thinking, for encouraging drawing, painting and the use of props and puppets and for organising events based around the main theme. You might like to create a word wall with the children or develop a word game whereby children match the words to objects. Even very young children respond positively when they see their ideas reflected back to them, so creating a wall of special words, displaying their creations in attractive ways and encouraging them to write their own versions of the rhymes and stories in a book will all reflect and illuminate their learning.

Some children, and in particular those who are less confident, find it very difficult to respond to a rhyme or story in a group situation. If the events of a story have moved them, they might not be able to talk about it and you should obviously respect their silence. Other children find listening very difficult, particularly if you choose a rhyme or story with no pictures or props. They might have rarely experienced the pleasure and rewards of listening to a story unfold, or joining in with a rhyme, and you might have to be very patient and try to make a link between a rhyme and story and a particular child's interests, so they begin to feel that their horizons are widening. Talking and sharing the children's responses will help them to engage with their own ideas, so ask questions like: *Do you remember another story where something like this happened? Which animal in the story do you like best? What do you think might happen next? Has anything like this happened to you? Did anything in the story frighten you?* As the children think about the answers to these sorts of questions, they will begin to reflect more deeply on the events, places and people in the rhyme or the story and make connections with other rhymes and stories they know. It is likely that the children's responses will vary and in this case you will need to follow their ideas wherever they might lead. Remember too that you are a model for the children, so join in with their conversation and show them that you are also thinking carefully about what happens in a particular story or rhyme: *My favourite part of the story is when Teeny Tiny Monkey shouts at the crocodile…* or *I remember my daddy telling me this story when I was little.*

Using outdoor spaces for inspiration

It is valuable for children to be outdoors in all weathers, so try to make use of your playground, nursery, school garden or playing field area to extend your rhyme and story space. In many of the chapters in Part II, we have made suggestions for taking the children outdoors to encourage different forms of learning. The outdoor atmosphere of freedom, light and space can encourage humour and playfulness more than indoor spaces. Some rhymes and stories lend themselves to the outdoor experience. On many occasions, our students used Michael Rosen and Helen Oxenbury's well-loved picture-story book We're Going on a Bear Hunt (1989) to help their children explore the outdoor environment while they tried to find the bear. In wet weather, children enjoy jumping in puddles and making a splash, so take them outside and invent your own splashy rhymes: *Splash, splash, went the raindrops, Splash, splash in the splishy-splashy puddles.* According to Tovey (2007), it is important for children to simply feel gleeful and delighted and marching across the play area to We're Going on a Bear Hunt or *This is the way we stamp our feet* will provide such joyful moments. These happy experiences are catchy, and soon spread to other children in the group, so they help to stimulate interest in those children who struggle to listen and hang back from joining in with sharing rhymes and stories indoors.

Some parents and teachers actively encourage children to focus on the natural world when they share rhymes and stories. If it is not possible to take the children outside, you might choose to bring the natural world into the classroom by growing plants and making a display of branches, leaves or picked produce to adorn your room, making the spaces welcoming and attractive. This use of objects from the natural world throughout each season complements the rhythms of young children's lives and at the same time makes the indoor space welcoming and attractive to children and their families.

In Denmark, the child's environment is developed in a holistic way, in consideration of children's physical, emotional and aesthetic well-being (Williams-Siegfredsen, 2012). For example, babies rest outdoors, in well-protected cots. This allows them opportunities to smell the smells and hear the sounds of nature in different seasons, such as the cutting of grass, bird song, the scent of flowers or the rustling of leaves. You might set up sleeping areas for babies and very young children under the trees or establish a routine with the same layout of rest mats and cots so that children can find their own places to rest and relax. You could provide baskets or other containers nearby so that children can get their own clothes and special objects when they wake up (Manning-Morton and Thorp, 2003). When the children are resting, take the opportunity to chant or sing to them. Ask parents to teach you the lullabies they sing so that you can sing them too. If their heads are on a pillow and their eyes are closed, they won't be able to see you, so think carefully about what they are hearing and how they might react to your voice and the rhythm of your speech.

Making time to reflect

It is worth developing a journal or log to make a collection of the rhymes and stories you are invited to use in this book, noting what has worked well and what you might want to change in the future. We encourage you to add more stories and rhymes that you can enjoy with the children. Reflect on your teaching and build your own collection of rhymes, stories and ideas to support children's healthy development.

Teachers as researchers

As a teacher, you engage in ongoing action research. You evaluate the learning and teaching that takes place on a daily basis, reflect on it and identify what you might do differently next time or what you might stop or start doing so that the learning is deeper or more sustained in the future. As a teacher, you are a researcher. Your findings are useful to you and the children you serve in the present.

You might be part of a learning group in your setting or school, whereby you and some colleagues identify questions, that is, what you want to find out and observe the learning that takes place in each other's contexts. You will discuss the learning in your groups. We encourage you to be such a researcher. Take up any opportunities to collaborate with colleagues within and beyond your setting. You might align yourself to an initiative with the local authority or with a university or college of higher education.

This is practical research. You know what you need to find out from one day to the next, so you plan what to do, evaluate how your teaching went, reflect on it and plan next steps. You collaborate with others to enrich the learning. Ultimately, we hope that you might be inspired to continue with your studies in some way and find out more about how this rhyming and storying approach supports young children's learning and development. We encourage you to be a lifelong learner, communicate your findings and spread your enthusiasm for this approach.

Concluding notes

So, now it is time for you to become a reciter and creator of rhymes, and a teller and inventor of stories.

In Part I, we discussed Bruner's assertion that children learn language by using it in social contexts. He puts this neatly:

Achieving joint reference is achieving a kind of solidarity with somebody.

(Bruner, 1987, p. 87)

We hope you will begin to achieve this solidarity by setting up a community of listeners for whom you are the reciter and creator of rhymes and the teller and inventor of stories. As your confidence grows, you will become a rhyme and story collector, attentive to texts, sounds and patterns that you can borrow to build your literary bank. Sarah found it useful to collect such pieces on cards in a box. You might find other ways to store your finds so that you can access them easily.

Your growing repertoire of rhymes and stories will reflect your experiences and those of the children, families and communities you serve. We invite you now to be creative together and to foster a sense of wonder. Perhaps the last word should go to the great storyteller Mary Medlicott:

Try it. Tell it. It is unlikely that you will regret it.

(2006, p. 38)

References

Bruner, J.S. (1987), The Transactional Self. In: Bruner, J.S. & Weinreich-Haste, H. eds. *Making Sense: The Child's Construction of the World*. London: Routledge: 81–96.

Department for Education (DfE). (2021), *Statutory Framework for the Early Years Foundation Stage. Setting the Standards for Learning, Development and Care for Children from Birth to Five*. https://www.gov.uk/government/publications

Department for Education (DfE). (2021), *The Reading Framework: Teaching the Foundations of Literacy. Guidance for Schools to Meet Existing Expectations for Teaching Early Reading*. http://www.gov.uk/government/publications

Edwards, P.E., Cline, K., Gandini, L., Giacomelli, A., Giovannini, D. & Galardini, A. (2014), Books, Stories, and the Imagination at "The Nursery Rhyme": A Qualitative Case Study of a Preschool Learning Environment in Pistoia, Italy, *Journal of Research in Childhood Education*, 28 (18–42), doi: 10.1080/02568543.2013.850131 [12 February 2021].

Lessing, D. (2007), Nobel Prize for Literature: Acceptance Speech. *The Guardian*, 8 December.

Manning-Morton, J. & Thorp, M. (2003), *Key Times for Play: The First Three Years*, Buckingham: McGraw-Hill Education.

Medlicott, M. (2006), *Tell It: A Practical Guide to Storytelling with Children Across the Primary Age-Range*. London: a storyworks publication.

Nutbrown, C. (2011), *Threads of Thinking: Schemas and Young Children's Learning*. 4th edn. London: Sage.

Rosen, M. & Oxenbury, H. (1989), *We're Going on a Bear Hunt*. London: Walker Books.

Tovey, H. (2007), *Playing Outdoors: Spaces and Places, Risk and Challenge*. Maidenhead: Open University Press.

Williams-Siegfredsen, J. (2012), *Understanding the Danish Forest School Approach: Early Years Education and Practice*. London: Routledge.

Part II Rhymes and stories

Boots and shoes

DOI: 10.4324/9781003358633-6

Overarching themes

- Using different materials for protection, for example rubber and leather

- Sharing skills with others

- Giving time to help others

- Appreciating the functions and uses of money and the importance of budgeting

Glossary

cobbler – a person who mends shoes
dame – an old-fashioned term for a woman
elves – small and friendly mythical creatures, only found in stories
fiddling-stick – the bow used to make music on a stringed instrument, for example violin
gentleman – a man, especially someone who has got a lot of money
hammer-man – someone who uses a hammer and other small tools to make or mend things
shoemaker – a person who makes shoes
workbench – a strong table used for making things on by hand or with tools

RHYMES

Introduce the main theme

Young children love to look at your shoes and show you their own. Make a collection of different kinds of boots and shoes. You may be able to find some unusual ones in charity shops or jumble sales. Invite the children to talk about the size, the shape, the colours and the texture of their own shoes and those that you've collected. Discuss shoes that are made for particular purposes – for example, ballet shoes, running shoes, mountaineering boots, trainers, football boots, slippers, and bootees for babies. What makes these shoes special? Draw and paint boots and shoes and make a display of shoes around your room. Include a selection of shoes from around the world if you can.

Rhyme 1

Rap-a-tap-a-rap-a-tap
Rap-a-tap-a-tap-a-tap
A-tick-a-tack-a-too!
A busy little hammer-man
Is mending up a shoe.

He sews the button on
With his teeny, tiny needle,
And, rap-a-tap-a-rap-a-tap,
A tick-a-tack-a-teedle.

Rhyme 2

Cobbler, cobbler, *mend my shoe*
Cobbler, cobbler, mend my shoe,
Get it done by half-past two,
If half past two can't be done,
Get it done by half-past one.

Enjoy the rhymes together

Chant "Rap-a-tap-a-rap-a-tap" and "Cobbler, cobbler, mend my shoe" orally, or if you prefer, write them up on a whiteboard so that the children can see the words. Chant or read the rhymes over and over again, encouraging the children to join in or to take over the reading from you. Mime the actions of hammering and sewing together and looking for something that has been lost. As you read, emphasise the rhymes and the repeated phrases in the texts: *too-shoe, needle-teedle, shoe-two.* Pause just before the rhyming word so that the children can anticipate and join in. Ask the children to clap the rhythm or use percussion instruments to make the sound of the hammer-man and the cobbler mending the shoes.

Talk about "the busy little hammer-man". Who is he? What is he doing? What does he look like? Ask the children what happens when their own shoes need mending.

Talk about the cobbler. Who might be asking him to mend a shoe? Why is this person in such a hurry to have their shoe mended?

Early literacy

Left to right sequencing

Use an enlarged copy of the rhymes and run your finger along each line to demonstrate left-to-right sequencing. Provide some sewing cards whereby children stitch from left to right.

Phonological awareness

Rhyme 1: look closely at the spelling patterns: Rap-a-Tap (*rap-tap, tick-tack, needle-teedle*), pointing out the initial sound(s), the phonic patterns and the word endings.

Encourage children to suggest other words and made-up words to add to the rhyming patterns with non-sensical words (e.g. rap, tap, map, lap, gap, and pap).

Rhyme 2: Cobbler, cobbler concentrate on the digraph "sh" in shoe. Point this out to the children and think of other words or names that begin or end with this digraph (e.g. *sh*ed, *Sh*eila, *sh*op, wi*sh*, and fi*sh*).

Make a collection of "sh" words. Invite the children to find other "sh" objects or bring some from home. Set up a shoe shine area where children can brush shoes.

Re-present the rhymes

Invite the children to draw or paint their own shoes, and talk about the colour of the shoes and what they are used for (dancing? walking? doing PE? playing football?). Label the different parts (e.g. sole, heel, laces, and tongue). Make these drawings into a wall display.

Playful maths

Introduce the concept of a pair, for example a pair of hands and a pair of eyes. Take an interest in children's shoes. Ah! Rosie is wearing red shoes! One red shoe and two red shoes. Ask the children to find out how many pairs of shoes their family members have. Add the numbers together. How many pairs of shoes are there altogether?

Play sorting games with shoes. Ask children wearing sandals, or blue shoes, or Velcro shoes to jump into the hoop, for example.

Set up a shoe shop. Put out some rulers, shoe boxes, a sales desk, and other suitable role play items. Organise shoes into different sizes or prices.

Use a clock face to help children learn to tell the time in *Cobbler, Cobbler,* focusing particularly on where the hands will be at half-past the hour.

Make a recording

Record yourselves chanting the rhymes together. Invite children or small groups of children to record each other and play back their recordings to the group. Listen to the recording together.

Ideas to inspire very young children

Play finger or toe rhymes like "This little pig went to market" if your children enjoy these.

Rhyme 3

Cock-a-doodle-doo
Cock-a-doodle-doo,
My dame has lost her shoe,
My master's lost his fiddling-stick,
Sing cock-a-doodle doo.

Chant the rhyme over and over again with the children.

Help the children to "feel" the rhythm of this rhyme by putting stress on the key words in each line (*Cock*-a-doodle-*do,* My *dame* has *lost* her *shoe*). Invite the children to clap in time to the rhythm.

Point to the children's shoes and say "Shoes" as you do, perhaps adding a colour – "black shoes, brown shoes, white shoes" and so on. Use your voice and eyes to connect with the children. These playful opportunities help to build relationships with you and the children. Invite parents to your rhyme and story session and share this game with the parents.

Foster a love of nature

Put on wellington boots and play jumping games, making noises on different surfaces as you land with two feet. Encourage children to jump into puddles and experience the splash.

It is valuable for children to simply feel delighted and joyous with you. Outdoor experiences such as these can lead to such moments. These happy experiences are catchy and soon spread to other children in the group. The outdoor atmosphere of freedom, light and space can encourage humour and playfulness more than indoor spaces.

STORY: THE ELVES AND THE SHOEMAKER

There was once an old shoemaker who lived with his wife in a little house. The shoemaker was very clever with his hands and he made the most beautiful shoes for babies, children, gentlemen and ladies. But even though he was very clever, the shoemaker sometimes didn't sell any shoes for weeks on end, and as you can imagine, he and his wife were very poor and sometimes they hardly had anything to eat.

One day, the shoemaker found that he only had enough leather to make one more pair of shoes. He couldn't afford to buy any more leather. He felt very sad, and he spent the afternoon cutting out the last pair of shoes with his strong scissors. Then, he put the leather on his workbench ready to make into shoes the next day. "It's a very sad day," he said to his wife, "but there's nothing to be done about it. I'll make this last pair of shoes in the morning and, you never know, a rich gentlemen might see them in the window and buy them." "Let's hope so," said his wife.

Early next morning, the shoemaker and his wife had some porridge for breakfast, and then, the shoemaker got ready to sew his very last pair of shoes. Imagine his surprise when he went to his workbench and saw a beautiful pair of shoes, all finished and waiting for someone to buy them! "Look!" he said to his wife. "How has this happened?" "I don't know," she said, "but I tell you what, they're beautifully made." His wife put the boots in the shop window to see if anyone might be interested in buying them.

Later that morning, a rich gentlemen came by on his horse. He noticed the beautiful shoes and came into the shop to try them on. "They're the most comfortable shoes I've ever worn!" he said. "I'll take them!" He was so pleased with the shoes that he gave the shoemaker twice as much money as he asked for. And so, now the shoemaker's wife could buy some more food and the shoemaker had enough money to buy the leather to make *two* pairs of shoes! That evening, he cut out the shoes and left the leather on his workbench ready to sew up the next day.

The next morning, the shoemaker and his wife had their porridge for breakfast, and then, the shoemaker went to his workbench to set to work. But, guess what? Both pairs of shoes were already finished. They were shiny and beautiful. "Whoever has done this?" asked the shoemaker's wife as she put the shoes in the shop window.

Two customers bought the shoes that morning, and they were so pleased with them that they gave the shoemaker twice as much money as he asked for, so he was able to go to market and buy enough leather to make four pairs of shoes. He cut these out ready to sew the next day but – guess what? – the next morning, he found that someone had finished them! And so, it went on. Every day, the shoemaker was able to buy more leather and cut the shoes out, and the next morning, the shoes were finished.

That evening when the shoemaker and his wife were eating their supper, the shoemaker's wife said, "I think it's time we found out who's helping us. Why don't we hide behind the sofa and see if we can see who's sewing these shoes, so that we can say thank you." "What a good idea," said the shoemaker. So that night, instead of going to bed, the shoemaker and his wife hid behind the sofa and kept very still.

When the clock struck 12, the shoemaker and his wife heard a little noise. Was it mice they could hear? When they saw what it was, their eyes grew wide with amazement. Two little elves had squeezed under the door, and then they climbed up the table leg on to the workbench. They worked all night, stitching away and making the shoes look neat and tidy, and they carried on till all the shoes were finished. Then, they climbed down the table leg and ran away under the door.

"I've never seen anything like it," said the shoemaker. "We must say thank you to those little elves." "Did you see how thin their clothes were?" said his wife. "They were shivering with cold. I have an idea. Let's make them some warm clothes." "That's a splendid idea," said the shoemaker. So, all the next day, the shoemaker's wife sewed and stitched. She made jackets and trousers for the elves, and then she made them some warm stockings and caps, and the shoemaker made them some beautiful shoes.

That night, the shoemaker and his wife didn't leave any shoes on the workbench. Instead, they left the new clothes there and then they hid behind the sofa to see what would happen. When the clock struck 12, the two little elves squeezed under the door and climbed up the table leg to the workbench. They looked for some shoes to sew, but there was none there. Instead, the elves found two beautiful suits of clothes all ready for them to wear. The shoemaker and his wife heard the little elves laughing and humming to themselves as they got dressed in their new clothes. "Thank you! Thank you!" they called out in their tiny voices as they climbed down the table leg and squeezed under the door.

And do you know, those little elves never came back, but they didn't need to, because thanks to their kindness, their hard work and their beautiful stitching, the shoemaker and his wife were never poor or hungry again.

Ways of telling

Read or tell the story to the children. Use your face and voice expressively to indicate suspense and surprise, and experiment with a different tone of voice for the shoemaker and his wife and for the tiny elves. Use mime from time to time, indicating the acts of cutting out and sewing, eating breakfast and crouching behind the sofa.

Early literacy

Stimulate talk

Invite the children to visualise what is happening in the story. Talk about what the elves are doing and how they are dressed. Where did the elves come from? Why did the elves help the old man and his wife? What might have happened to the shoemaker and his wife if the elves had not helped them? What would you have done to thank the elves?

Reading

Make a collection of different versions of the story and other stories about shoes.

Creative writing

Invite the children to write or type their own rhyme or story about shoes. Make a book for everyone to read.

Encourage creativity

Visual re-presentations

Ask the children to draw or paint their own picture from their favourite part of the story. Make a display and ask each child to tell you about their picture.

Role play

Provide small world people and objects in the sand tray or outdoors to encourage children to develop their own versions of the story. Participate in children's play, weaving in particular vocabulary to support their communication development.

If you are working with older children, invite them to work in groups of four to tell their own story of the Elves and the Shoemaker. They could perform their play to everyone else in the class.

Hot seat yourself as one of the elves or as the shoemaker or his wife and invite the children to ask you questions about your life.

Playful maths

Talk about the shoemaker and his wife's financial situation before the elves helped them. Suggest that the children do some sums to help them with their budgeting.

Provide calculators, counting objects, pads of paper, writing implements and other resources to encourage children to talk about, recognise and write numbers.

Link to a published book

Mr. Magnolia by Quentin Blake

First published in 1980, this exquisite rhyming picture book has an obvious link with this chapter. "Mr. Magnolia has only one boot" is the oft-repeated and highly literary phrase that appears throughout. The text and illustrations are clever, witty and charming, so there is plenty to talk about. And there is an air of mystery. One day, a strange parcel arrives for Mr. Magnolia. Where did it come from? What can be in it? Did the elves have something to do with it?

2 Baking bread

DOI: 10.4324/9781003358633-7

Rhymes and stories in this chapter

- Rhyme 1: I went into the baker's shop
- Rhyme 2 for the very young: Pat-a-cake, pat-a-cake
- Story: The Little Red Hen

Overarching themes

- Sharing resources with others

- Understanding the role of law and the justice system in our society

- Caring for the environment

Glossary

appetising – tasty and delicious

ears of corn – a tall shoot with long leaves tightly packed around lots of yellow kernels of corn

grain – edible seeds, for example corn or wheat, found on plants

mill – a building near water with large wheels used to grind the grain

miller – the person who works at the mill

"shrugged her shoulders" – the Little Red Hen raises and lowers her shoulders as a way of saying there is nothing she can do about the animals who are refusing to help her

scoop – gather grain in handfuls or spoonfuls

RHYMES

Introduce the main theme

The children in your setting might not have seen wheat growing, so try to get some or, at any rate, show them a picture of wheat, pointing out the grains. Show them flour too and explain how it's made from the grains of wheat. If you can, bake some bread with the children and then enjoy eating it.

Rhyme 1

I went into the baker's shop

I went into the baker's shop

To buy a loaf of bread, bread, bread,
He wrapped it in a five-pound note
And this is what he said, said, said...
My name is I doe I doe
Wee Willy Whiskers
Chinese chopsticks,
Merci.

Enjoy the rhyme together

Chant the rhyme to the children (if you can, learn it by heart so that you can keep eye contact with the group), or write it up on a whiteboard or a large piece of paper, so the children can see the words. Chant or read the rhyme over and over again, encouraging the children to join in or to take over the reading from you.

Bring the rhyme to life with actions and sounds. Mime the actions as you go along: swing your arms as you walk into the baker's shop and wrap up the bread. Clap your hands as you say "bread, bread, bread" and "said, said, said". Make up a clapping game for the children.

Show the children a five-pound note and explain that many years ago these notes were much bigger and so you would have been able to use one to wrap a loaf in.

Early literacy

Use the rhyme and rhythm

As you read, emphasise the rhyme and the repeated words: *said* and *bread*. Pause just before these two repeated words and encourage the children to anticipate the rhyme and join in with you.

The second four lines introduce a different rhythm, with an emphasis on these words or syllables: *name*, *I*, *Wee*, *Whis*, *Chin*, *chop* and *Mer*. It is worth practising these lines before you say them aloud with the children, so you feel confident.

Play with the language

The lines "I doe, I doe, Wee Willy Whiskers, Chinese chopsticks, Merci" make no sense but are great fun to say aloud. Chant them over and over again with the children and enjoy the sounds together. Explain that "merci" is French for "thank you". If you have children and other colleagues who speak languages other than English, ask them how they say "thank you" in their own language. Write these words down and make a Thank you rhyme of your own. Practise saying your invented rhyme together and perform it for the other children or for parents. Make a recording of the children chanting the "thank you" rhyme.

Phonological awareness

If you have the rhyme written down, say the initial sounds *b*, *s*, *w* and the grapheme *ch*. Ask the children to identify the words beginning with these letters.

Write a Thank you book

Write the words *Thank you* in a variety of languages in your book and ask the children to illustrate each use of *Thank you* with a typical person or scene from that country. Word process the book and put it in the class library for everyone to read and share.

Encourage role play

If you can, take the children to a local bakery to look at the different kinds of bread on sale. Turn a corner of your room into a baker's shop. Help the children to make a sign that will hang over the shop, together with the opening hours, and a list of the different kinds of bread and how much each sort will cost. Collect paper bags or provide a roll of brown paper for packaging the bread. Make different kinds of bread from playdough or other materials. As a special treat, use real bread. Invite each class to come and buy your bread. If there are parents in your setting who work in a bread shop or bakery, or who enjoy making bread, ask them if they could demonstrate bread-making for the children.

Playful maths

Price the loaves in the bakery role play area. Encourage children to read and write numbers as part of their play. Join in with children's play and model mathematical language to support their understanding of mathematical vocabulary, for example, *one more, altogether.*

Ideas to inspire very young children

Rhyme 2

> *Pat-a-cake pat-a-cake*
> Pat-a-cake, pat-a-cake baker's man
> Bake me a cake as fast as you can
> Pat it and prick it and mark it with B
> And put it in the oven for baby and me

For baby and me
For baby and me
Put it in the oven for baby and me.

Hold the child and make mouth movements as you chant the words of the rhyme. Say each word clearly as you look at the child. Encourage the child to join in and respond to their mouth movements. Take your time and have fun.

Share sensory experiences, as appropriate, depending on the age of the child. Allow children to explore and taste small chunks of bread with their hands and mouths. Make some dough for older children to manipulate. Bake bread so that children can smell fresh bread.

STORY: THE LITTLE RED HEN

Little Red Hen lived on a farm. Every morning after breakfast she went for a walk round the farmyard. When she met the other animals, she always greeted them by saying, "Chook chook."

"Chook chook," she said to the goose.
"Chook chook," she said to the cat.
"Chook chook," she said to the pig.
"Good morning, Little Red Hen," they said, and then they went on their way.

One morning, it was extremely hot and the farmer decided to cut the wheat in his field. He brought the wheat into his farmyard and put it in the barn to keep it dry. Little Red Hen noticed that some of the grains of wheat had been scattered around the farmyard, and so she scooped the grains up in her beak. "I can grow these and make some delicious bread with them!" she thought. "Will anyone help me plant these grains of wheat?" she asked. But everyone seemed to be too busy.

"Not I," said the goose.
"Not I," said the cat.
"Not I," said the pig.

Little Red Hen shrugged her shoulders. "Very well," she said, "I'll have to do it all by myself." And that's exactly what she did. When she'd finished planting the wheat, she asked: "Will anyone help me water the grains of wheat?" But everyone seemed to be too busy.

"Not I," said the goose.
"Not I," said the cat.
"Not I," said the pig.

Little Red Hen shrugged her shoulders. "Very well," she said, "I'll have to do it all by myself." And that's exactly what she did.

Every day Little Red Hen watched her plants growing taller and taller. At last, the ears of corn were ripe and she decided it was time to cut them. "Will anyone help me cut the wheat?" she asked. But everyone seemed to be too busy.

"Not I," said the goose.
"Not I," said the cat.
"Not I," said the pig.

Little Red Hen shrugged her shoulders. "Very well," she said, "I'll have to do it all by myself." And that's exactly what she did. When Little Red Hen had cut the wheat, she had to shake the stems to loosen the grains of corn. "Will anyone help shake the wheat to get the grains out?" she asked. But everyone seemed to be too busy.

"Not I," said the goose.
"Not I," said the cat.
"Not I," said the pig.

Little Red Hen shrugged her shoulders. "Very well," she said, "I'll have to do it all by myself." And that's exactly what she did. She shook and shook the wheat until she had a large pile of grain. "Now, I need to take all this grain to the miller so he can grind it into flour," she said. "Will anyone help me put the grain into a sack?" she asked. But everyone seemed to be too busy.

"Not I," said the goose.
"Not I," said the cat.
"Not I," said the pig.

Little Red Hen shrugged her shoulders. "Very well," she said, "I'll have to do it all by myself." And that's exactly what she did. She carried the heavy sack to the mill, and the miller ground the grains of wheat into flour. Little Red Hen took it back to the farm. "Now, I'm going to bake a beautiful loaf of bread," she said. "Will anyone help me bake the bread?" she asked. But everyone seemed to be too busy.

"Not I," said the goose.
"Not I," said the cat.
"Not I," said the pig.

Little Red Hen shrugged her shoulders. "Very well," she said, "I'll have to do it all by myself." And that's exactly what she did. When she took the loaf of bread out of the oven, it smelled very appetising.

"Mmm," said the goose.
"Mmm," said the cat.
"Mmm," said the pig.

Little Red Hen spread butter over the bread. "Now, who will help me eat the bread?" she said.

"I will!" said the goose.
"I will!" said the cat.
"I will!" said the pig.

"Oh, I don't think so," said Little Red Hen. "None of you helped me before, so why should I share my loaf of bread with you? I'm going to eat it all by myself." And that's exactly what she did.

Ways of telling

Tell your own version of the story or read this version to the children, encouraging them to join in with the repeated phrases, such as *Not I*; *I'll have to do it all by myself*; *And that's exactly what she did*. If you like, invent different voices or accents for the hen, the goose, the cat and the pig. If you're using puppets, choose four children to hold the animal puppets and invite them to say their individual lines and shake their heads when they say, "Not I."

Early literacy

Non-fiction

Make a collection of baking books and baking items, for example bags of flour and packets of yeast, for them to read. Invite families to bring in their favourite baking recipes.

Writing

Invite the children to retell the story in their own words and to illustrate their story. Share these stories with the group and put them into a class book so everyone can read them over and over again.

Older children could write a letter to your local supermarket bakery, asking for information about how they make bread. This is a good opportunity to show children how to set a letter out (address, contact details and appropriate endings – e.g. *Regards* and *Yours sincerely*) and to insist that the letter is perfect in every way because it's being sent to a real person who will read it carefully.

Use of language

Draw attention to some of the verbs, adverbs and adjectives used in the story: *scattered, scooped, delicious, appetising, extremely* and the phrase *shrugged her shoulders*. Encourage the children to talk about the meaning of these words and to use them in their own re-tellings of the story.

Set up a bread tasting area and invite children to use different words to describe the taste and texture of the bread. Build up a bank of bread tasting adjectives.

Foster a love of nature

Outing to a farm

If possible, organise a visit to a local farm where children can see the hens and chickens.

Incubate eggs and raise chickens

Schools and nurseries can borrow an incubator and raise chickens from eggs. This experience helps the children to learn a variety of skills – turning the eggs regularly, knowing when the chicks are ready to hatch, caring for the chicks and so on. This is a big responsibility for the nursery or school community. Make sure that the chicks can thrive in your setting.

Playful maths

Make bread with the children. Talk about the measurements and quantities you need and help them gain mathematical fluency as you guide them through the process. Use vocabulary such as:

- heavy/light, heavier than or lighter than
- full/empty, more than, less than, half, half full or quarter

Encourage creativity

If possible, show the children pictures of a farmyard, a windmill, grains of wheat, a pig, a goose, a cat and a hen. Encourage the children to look closely at each one, as you point out the main features – the shape, the colour, the size and the expressions on their faces. Ask the children to draw or paint their favourite part of the story. Share the drawings and paintings with the whole group. Make a display of the story with speech bubbles showing "Not I…" and read these together.

Role play

Use hand puppets or make cardboard puppets to represent the Little Red Hen, the goose, the cat and the pig. Use the puppets to help you to tell the story and then invite the children to re-enact the story themselves with the puppets. Older children could write their own playscript.

Collect small world creatures and objects for children to re-enact the story and develop it through play. Observe the children as they play so that you can encourage and support them in the moment. As a rule, this is more valuable than standing back and writing observations.

Involve parents as much as possible in your work. Encourage them to tell you how their children continue acting out the story at home or bring things in to support the play at the nursery or school.

Link to a published book

Rosie's Walk by Pat Hutchins

The Little Red Hen is famous for baking bread, but perhaps the most famous hen of all is Rosie. Rosie's Walk was first published over 50 years ago, and it is still one of the most well-loved picture books of all time. Rosie the hen goes for a walk around the farmyard pursued by a wily fox whose presence spells danger.

The fox might be clever, but he is also clumsy. He steps on a garden rake, falls in the pond, smashes into the haycock (a good old-fashioned term), covers himself with flour from the mill and upsets the beehives. Interestingly, none of these disasters is told to readers through the text. Every one of his misfortunes is shown in the illustrations, and so this is an ideal book for helping children to derive meaning from the pictures and to laugh at the fox's mishaps too.

Rosie's Walk is therefore an ideas book for promoting discussion. Does Rosie know the fox is there? Has she perhaps set these traps for him? And what would the Little Red Hen in our story have done if she had known there was a fox in the farmyard waiting to pounce?

Rosie's Walk can also be used to explore the use of a variety of pronouns – *across, around, over, past, through* or *under*. A knowledge of these pronouns will be of particular value for children who are learning English as an additional language.

Left-right sequencing and page turning are also encouraged through both text and illustration.

3 Growing things

DOI: 10.4324/9781003358633-8

Rhymes and stories in this chapter

- Rhyme 1: Oats and beans and barley grow
- Rhyme 2 for the very young: Five little peas in a pea-pod pressed
- Rhyme 3 for the very young: I had a little marigold seed
- Rhyme 4 for the very young: Flowers grow like this
- Story: The enormous turnip

Overarching themes

- Caring for nature

- Growing things

- Sharing produce with others

Glossary

barley – a plant grown by farmers, used to make beer and for feeding to animals

beans – small seeds that often grow in pods. "Baked beans" or "beans on toast" will probably be familiar to the children, but you can explain that there are other kinds of beans that farmers grow in fields

dusted – "dusted themselves down" – tidied themselves up

ease – "takes his ease" – the farmer is resting after doing all the hard work of sowing the seeds

oats – a plant grown by farmers, used in porridge and for feeding to animals

tabby – a tabby cat has brown fur with dark stripes

RHYMES

Introduce the main theme

Talk to the children about the plants they see growing around them, indoors, in their garden or on their way to school or nursery. If you have trees and flowers in your setting, encourage the children to observe and describe them. Do they have a favourite flower? Why is this? Is it to do with the colour or the smell? Make a collection of flowers and things about planting in your room.

Rhyme 1

Oats and beans and barley grow
Oats and beans and barley grow,
Oats and beans and barley grow,
But not you nor I nor anyone knows,
How oats and beans and barley grow.

First the farmer sows his seed,
Then he stands and takes his ease,
Stamps his feet and claps his hands,
And turns around to view the land.

Enjoy the rhyme together

Chant or sing "Oats and beans and barley grow" repeatedly, as part of your daily routine, encouraging the children to join in, clapping the rhythm and shaking their heads when they say "But not you nor I nor anyone knows".

Chant the second verse of the rhyme "First the farmer sows his seed." Stand in a circle to mime the movements for sowing, standing at ease, stamping feet, clapping hands and turning round.

Encourage creativity

Encourage the children to listen to the rhythm of each rhyme, clapping their hands in time to the pulse and keeping the beat with a drum, a triangle or a guiro. Children enjoy marching to the beat. Use your outdoor space, if possible, to recite and move to the rhyme.

Foster a love of nature

Young children love to plant seeds and bulbs, watching them grow and learning to take care of them. Depending on the time of year, plant sunflower or wild flower seeds or bulbs in a window box or even in a small garden outside your nursery or classroom and encourage the children to take care of them.

Playful maths

Cook with the children and their families. Use the cooking opportunity to develop mathematical fluency. Provide a range of containers and implements and place them in a tray of barley or other grain. Carry out appropriate risk assessments before using any small, edible pieces. Use water instead of grain if necessary.

Layer on mathematical vocabulary as children fill and pour the grain in and out of different-sized containers. Children progress from using and comparing different types of quantities using non-standard units to using common standard units.

Try to get some oats, beans and barley. Make some porridge and enjoy eating it with the children. Cook baked beans and eat them on toast. Make barley soup. Provide clipboards and other writing materials. Some children might want to write down the ingredients and the recipes and take them home to their families.

Invite families to share their ideas for cooking with the children. They might want to bring in their favourite dishes to reflect different heritages.

Early literacy

Phonological awareness

Using the b sound from beans and barley, ask the children to think of other foods that begin with the initial sound b (e.g. baked beans, bacon, banana, bagel, baklava, biryani, blackcurrant, blueberry, bread, broad bean, broccoli, burger and butter). Make a list of the names they think of and read these together, emphasising the initial sound b. Collect as many of these foods as you can and display them with labels for each of their names.

Ideas to inspire very young children

Recite these finger rhymes together

Rhyme 2

Five little peas in a pea-pod pressed
Five little peas in a pea-pod pressed,
   Clench fingers on one hand.
One grew, two grew and so did all the rest.
   Raise fingers slowly.
They grew and grew and did not stop,
   Stretch fingers wide.
Until one day the pod went POP.
   Clap loudly when you say POP.

Rhyme 3

I had a little marigold seed
I had a little marigold seed.
   Mime holding a tiny seed between your thumb and forefinger.
I put it in a pot.
   Mime putting the seed in a pot.

I watered it and watered it with ginger pop.
  Raise your elbow and mime watering the seed.
It grew, and grew, and did not stop,
  Raise your arms high in the air.
Until one day the pod went POP!
  Clap your hands together.

Rhyme 4

Flowers grow like this
Flowers grow like this
  Cup hands.
Trees grow like this;
  Spread arms.
I grow just like this!
  Jump up and stretch.

STORY: THE ENORMOUS TURNIP

Once upon a time, an old man and his wife lived on a farm. They had a lot of animals to look after, so they were always very busy. Every year, they planted vegetables in their garden and watched them grow. "I know what we'll plant this year," said the farmer, "we'll plant a turnip seed! Just think of all the beautiful soup we can make from the turnip!"

So, the old man planted a turnip seed and every day he watered the seed. The sun shone down and warmed the ground, and before long, the old man and his wife saw green turnip leaves sprouting out of the ground. Soon the turnip was poking through the soil. They watched it grow ... and grow ... and grow. First, it was bigger than Tabby Kitten, then it was bigger than Brown Rabbit, then it was bigger than Mrs. Hen, then it was bigger than Spotty Dog, then it was bigger than Grey Donkey and then it was even bigger than Moo the Cow! "Look," said the old man, "now it's bigger than you and me! What shall we do?"

"We must pull it up now," said the old man's wife. "We can make lots of soup from it. Come on, you get hold of the leaves and pull." So, the old man pulled and pulled, but he couldn't pull the turnip up. "Let's both pull," said his wife. "I'll hold you round the middle." And so they pulled ... and pulled ... and pulled ... but they couldn't pull the turnip up.

"I know," said the old man's wife. "Let's ask Tabby Kitten to help us," and that's what they did. Tabby Kitten held on to the old man's wife and she held on to the old man, and they pulled ... and pulled ... and pulled ... but they couldn't pull the turnip up.

"I know," said the old man's wife. "Let's ask Brown Rabbit to help us," and that's what they did. Brown Rabbit held on to Tabby Kitten, Tabby Kitten held on to the old man's wife and she held on to the old man, and they pulled ... and pulled ... and pulled ... but they couldn't pull the turnip up.

"I know," said the old man's wife. "Let's ask Mrs. Hen to help us," and that's what they did. Mrs. Hen held on to Brown Rabbit, Brown Rabbit held on to Tabby Kitten, Tabby Kitten held on to the old man's wife and she held on to the old man, and they pulled ... and pulled ... and pulled ... but they couldn't pull the turnip up.

"I know," said the old man's wife. "Let's ask Spotty Dog to help us," and that's what they did. So, Spotty Dog held on to Mrs. Hen, Mrs. Hen held on to Brown Rabbit, Brown Rabbit held on to Tabby Kitten, Tabby Kitten held on to the old man's wife and she held on to the old man, and they pulled ... and pulled ... and pulled ... but they couldn't pull the turnip up.

"I know," said the old man's wife. "Let's ask Grey Donkey to help us," and that's what they did. So, Grey Donkey held on to Spotty Dog, Spotty Dog held on to Mrs. Hen, Mrs. Hen held on to Brown Rabbit, Brown Rabbit held on to Tabby Kitten, Tabby Kitten held on to the old man's wife and she held on to the old man, and they pulled ... and pulled ... and pulled ... but they couldn't pull the turnip up.

"I know," said the old man's wife. "Let's ask Moo the Cow to help us," and that's what they did. So, Moo the Cow held on to Grey Donkey, Grey Donkey held on to Spotty Dog, Spotty Dog held on to Mrs. Hen, Mrs. Hen held on to Brown Rabbit, Brown Rabbit held on to Tabby Kitten, Tabby Kitten held on to the old man's wife and she held on to the old man, and they pulled ... and pulled ... and pulled ... and the turnip came up at last!

And everyone tumbled over and fell on top of each other.
The old man fell on top of the old woman ...
The old woman fell on top of Tabby Kitten ...
Tabby Kitten fell on top of Brown Rabbit ...
Brown Rabbit fell on top of Mrs. Hen ...
Mrs. Hen fell on top of Spotty Dog ...
Spotty Dog fell on top of Grey Donkey ...
and Grey Donkey fell on top of Moo the Cow.

Thankfully, no one was hurt. They all got up, dusted themselves down and looked at the enormous turnip. "I've never seen such a huge turnip," said the old woman. "Come on, everybody, it's tea-time. I'll make us all a bowl of turnip soup!" And that's exactly what she did, so they all sat down and had a delicious meal.

Ways of telling

This story will really come to life if you involve the children, so encourage them to join in with you.

And so they pulled ... and pulled ... and pulled....

Do the actions too, extending your arms as you heave on the imaginary turnip. Try to learn the sequence so that you do not have to rely on the printed story. If you can, have a real turnip to show the children. Let them handle it, and talk about it too – the colour, the shape, the size – and perhaps you could make some turnip soup.

Early literacy

Encourage prediction

Prediction is an important reading strategy, so as you tell or read the story, pause before the repeated phrases (e.g. *And so they pulled … and pulled … and pulled … but they couldn't pull the turnip up*) and encourage the children to take over the storytelling. Use the same technique of pausing before introducing each animal in turn.

Write a book

Take photos of the children's drawings and paintings and put these into a class book. Invite the children to write parts of the story to accompany their pictures and then type and print their writing. Some children might want to type up their stories in the first instance and use the print function on the computer. Read the children's stories to the whole group and put the book into your class library for everyone to enjoy.

Encourage creativity

Re-present the story

Show the children pictures of the old man and his wife, the turnip, the kitten, the rabbit, the hen, the dog, the donkey and the cow and talk about their various characteristics. Encourage the children to look closely at each animal, as you point out the main features – the colour, the markings on the fur, the relative sizes, the expressions on their faces. Invite the children to draw or paint their favourite part of the story. Share the drawings and paintings with the whole group. Make a wall display of the story.

Role play

Collect figurines of each animal and the old man and old woman, and bring these out of a box or a bag, as each one joins with the others to pull on the turnip. Invite the children to retell the story in twos or threes, using the figurines to help them remember the sequence of events.

Foster a love of nature

Provide gardening tools and gloves and invite children to garden with you. Can they help you pull up the roots of dandelions? They might enjoy raking leaves, sweeping them and scooping them up into gardening recycling bins.

Playful maths

Use your favourite classroom or home puppets to tell the story of the Enormous Turnip and teach mathematical concepts, for example "one more". As *one more* character joins the effort to pull the turnip, their combined strength increases. Pose some story challenges, for example, How many more are needed to pull the turnip up? Two more? Three more?

Link to a published book

The Story of Johnny Appleseed by Aliki

We are sure the children will enjoy this story, published by Aladdin in 1971. It is widely available, and there are several versions on the Internet. Johnny Appleseed was an American pioneer who lived in the 1800s, and his real name was John Chapman. He collected apple seeds from across America, carried them in a sack and gave them to people so that they could grow their own apple orchards.

4 Crocodiles and monkeys

DOI: 10.4324/9781003358633-9

Rhymes and stories in this chapter

- Rhyme 1: The Swampy River Crocodile
- Rhyme 2 for the very young: Monkey, monkey, mangrove tree
- Rhyme 3 for the very young: One, two, three, four

Overarching themes

- Being frightened of the unknown and overcoming that fear

- Being clever and resourceful

- Learning that enemies can become friends

Glossary

mango – a tropical fruit, with yellow and red colouring
mangrove – a tree that grows in swampy areas
swamp – a damp place full of mud and water
wary – being careful if there is danger around
"stuff and nonsense" – a saying meaning "don't be silly" or "don't be foolish"

RHYMES

Introduce the main theme

These rhymes and the accompanying story draw on children's mixture of excitement and fear of darkness and mystery, exemplified by the mysterious jungle, the crocodile who is lying in wait for its next meal and the deep dark river that winds its way through the mangrove swamp. Underlying all these images is the fear of being chased and eaten up. But finally, the fear is taken away, and all ends happily.

Many children will have seen crocodiles and monkeys in wildlife films, story books or at the zoo. Invite them to describe these animals and to tell stories about them so that you build up a picture of their various characteristics.

Show the children pictures of crocodiles and monkeys or have puppets or toys as props. Talk about their characteristics – the crocodile's teeth, eyes and claws; the monkey's long arms and tail; and so on. Ask questions: Where have you seen these animals? – in the zoo or safari park or on television? What is special about them? What do they eat?

Rhyme I

The Swampy River Crocodile

The swampy river crocodile
Is very, very scary,
And if you look him in the eye,
You must be very wary.

The swampy river crocodile
Is very, very frightening,
You think he's slow, but watch him go –
He moves as fast as lightning.

The swampy river crocodile
Is very, very wild,
But talk to him gently and find
He's really soft inside.

You see, the swampy river crocodile
Is very, very sad,
You can hear him crying late at night,
"Everyone thinks I'm bad."

So if you see this crocodile
Do not shake and shiver,
Be sure to say you like him,
And you'll be friends forever.

Enjoy the rhyme together

Be expressive as you recite the rhyme. Use different tones of your voice and vary the pace and pitch of your delivery to indicate the feeling of being scared (slow and whispery), then the feeling of being sorry for the crocodile (a warm and gentle use of your voice.)

When you say "You think he's slow, but watch him go – he moves as fast as lightning," move your fingers slowly up your arm and then get faster and faster as they reach your shoulder. Use wide-open eyes to indicate "look him in the eye", and move your arms very quickly as if you were swimming to show the crocodile moving "as fast as lightning"; hug yourself to indicate "shake and shiver". If you are using a crocodile prop, look at it when you say "Look him in the eye" and invite the children to do the same.

Ideas to support very young children

Rhyme 2

Monkey, monkey, mangrove tree
Monkey, monkey, mangrove tree,
I will catch you, wait and see;
River deep or river wavy,
I'll eat you up with monkey gravy.

Rhyme 3

One, two, three, four
One, two, three, four,
Monkeys on the forest floor,
Five, six, seven, eight,
Eating mangoes off a plate.

Enjoy these rhymes together

Chant Monkey, monkey, mangrove tree. Encourage the children to join in as you repeat the rhyme. Ask the children who "I" is in the rhyme. Use your hands and arms to indicate the "wavy" river and at the end of the rhyme mime chewing your food.

Make One, two, three, four into a finger rhyme and encourage the children to join in. If you can, bring a mango in to show the children what this fruit looks like. Invite them to hold it, feel its weight and to talk about its size and colour. Cut the mango into portions and taste it. What does it taste like?

Re-present the rhymes

Invite the children to make their own illustrations of monkeys and crocodiles. Gather the pictures together and talk about them. Put them into a jungle picture with the river and the mangrove trees. Use captions from the rhymes on the picture, for example "River deep or river wavy"; "he moves as fast as lightning" and read these with the children. Copy the children's favourite rhymes and display these on the wall alongside the illustrations. Talk about the display and read the rhymes together.

Early literacy

Encourage prediction

In each rhyme, pause before you chant the rhyming word and invite the children to guess what it will be.

Phonological awareness

Rhyme 1: point out the consonant clusters (sw, cr, sc and fr) and the digraph (sh). Help the children to listen for these. Point to the words and think of other words that contain these clusters (e.g. *crack, crane, creak, crow* or *crying; swim, swan, switch,* or *swing*).

Rhymes 2 and 3: point out the initial sound "m" (monkey and mangrove) and collect other words beginning with "m." Highlight rhyming sounds and encourage children to suggest made-up or familiar rhyming words (e.g. *four, floor, door, more, core, bore, or tree, see, bee, fee, me, tea, sea*).

Introduce non-fiction publications

Generate questions about crocodiles and monkeys, then use information books, pamphlets or the Internet to find the answers.

Role play

Using the information you have gathered and choosing one or more rhymes, put together a presentation for other children in your school, home setting or nursery for families to enjoy together.

Playful maths

Use Rhyme 3 to develop counting. Choose 8 children to play the part of the monkeys. Give each of them a number to hold from 1 to 8 and ask the other children to count, pointing to each number as you go along the line.

STORY: THE MONKEYS AND THE CROCODILE

In the deep dark mangrove forests of Borneo, by the side of a warm and muddy river, there lived a family of monkeys: Father Monkey, Mother Monkey and Teeny-Tiny Monkey. They lived high in the branches of a mangrove tree, and they spent their days climbing up the trees and swinging through the branches, scratching where it itched the most, taking a nap in the middle of the day when it was very hot and picking the sweetest fruit and eating it all up. Mmmm ... lovely.

But someone else lived in the deep dark mangrove forests, by the side of the warm and muddy river: a huge crocodile. He spent his days looking for things to eat – fishes, crabs and, sometimes, monkeys.

One morning, the monkey family woke up, had a good stretch and climbed high into the branches of the mangrove tree to find some sweet fruits for their breakfast.

But the only ones left on the tree were dried up and they didn't taste nice. "I think we must have eaten all the good ones," said Mother Monkey. "What shall we do?"

"There's plenty over on the other side of the river," said Father Monkey. "I can see them growing on the tree."

"We'll have to swim over the river to get them," said Mother Monkey. "Come on. Let's go! I'm hungry."

"Not so fast!" said Father Monkey. "Let's think carefully about this." He looked very serious. "Remember the crocodile," he said. "He's very dangerous. You know what happened to your uncle last year." Mother Monkey nodded and she looked frightened.

"How many teeth has a crocodile got?" asked Teeny-Tiny Monkey. "Enough to bite you with and swallow you up whole," said his mother. She looked directly at her son. "If he catches you, he'll eat you up." Teeny-Tiny Monkey shivered, but then he looked at the ripe fresh fruits on the other side of the river and he said,

"Let me swim across to get the fruit. I'm a fast swimmer, and the crocodile would never catch me. And if I see him I'll shout:

Your teeth are ferocious,
You think you're the boss,
But you'll never stop me
From swimming across!"

"Bravo!" said Father Monkey. "You're very brave. Off you go!"

And so, Teeny-Tiny Monkey jumped into the water. He began to swim across the river, and he kept his eyes fixed on the mangrove tree on the other side, with all those wonderful fruits just waiting to be eaten.

Suddenly, he heard a loud splash behind him. "Who are you?" shouted the crocodile, "and what are you doing in my river?"

"I'm Teeny-Tiny Monkey," he said, "and this is NOT your river. It belongs to us all." And then he sang:

"Your teeth are ferocious,
You think you're the boss,
But you'll never stop me
From swimming across!"

"Stuff and nonsense!" shouted the crocodile.

"It isn't nonsense," said Teeny-Tiny Monkey. "I'm going to swim across and eat those fabulous fruits on the mangrove tree."

"Oh no, you're not," said the crocodile, "because I'm going to eat you all up!"

Teeny-Tiny Monkey thought very quickly. "Don't eat me," he said, "I'm far too small. Wait till my mother swims across. She's much bigger than me!"

"Very well," said the crocodile, and he sank slowly back into the water while Teeny-Tiny Monkey swam across to the other side. He clambered up the riverbank and climbed high up into the mangrove tree. He picked a delicious fruit and began to eat it all up. Mmmm ... it tasted wonderful.

Mother Monkey watched her son swim across. "My turn now," she said. She jumped into the river and began to swim across. She kept her eyes fixed on the big mangrove tree on the other side, with all those wonderful fruits, just waiting to be picked and eaten.

Suddenly, she heard a loud splash behind her. "Who are you?" shouted the crocodile, "and what are you doing in my river?"

"I'm Mother Monkey," she said, "and this is NOT your river. It belongs to us all." And then she sang:

"Your teeth are ferocious,
You think you're the boss,
But you'll never stop me
From swimming across!"

"Stuff and nonsense!" shouted the crocodile.

"It isn't nonsense," said Mother Monkey. "I'm going to swim across and eat those fabulous fruits on the mangrove tree."

"Oh no, you're not," said the crocodile, "because I'm going to eat you all up!"

Mother Monkey thought very quickly. "Don't eat me," she said, "I'm only medium-sized. Wait till Father Monkey swims across. He's much bigger than me!"

"Very well," said the crocodile, and he sank slowly back into the water while Mother Monkey swam across to the other side. She clambered up the riverbank and climbed high up into the mangrove tree. She gave Teeny-Tiny Monkey a big hug and then she picked a delicious fruit. Mmmm ... it tasted wonderful.

Father Monkey watched Mother Monkey swim across. "My turn now," he said. He jumped into the river and began to swim across. He kept his eyes fixed on the big mangrove tree on the other side, with all those wonderful fruits, just waiting to be eaten.

Suddenly, he heard a loud splash behind him. "Who are you?" shouted the crocodile, "and what are you doing in my river?"

"I'm Father Monkey," he said, "and this is NOT your river. It belongs to us all." And then he sang:

"Your teeth are ferocious,
You think you're the boss,
But you'll never stop me
From swimming across!"

"Stuff and nonsense!" shouted the crocodile.

"It isn't nonsense," said Father Monkey. "I'm going to swim across and eat those fabulous fruits on the mangrove tree."

"Oh no, you're not," said the crocodile, "because I'm going to eat you all up!"

"You'll have to catch me first!" said Father Monkey, and he began to swim as fast as he could, but the crocodile swam faster. The crocodile got nearer and nearer and nearer, and then he opened his mouth as wide as he could, showing all his dagger-like teeth. Suddenly, something hit him on the head. "Ouch!" he screamed. "Ouch! Ouch!"

He looked up. Teeny-Tiny Monkey and Mother Monkey were throwing the heavy mangrove fruits right on to the crocodile's head. "Please stop it!" he shouted to them. "Stop hitting me!"

"We'll stop hitting you if you let my daddy go!" shouted Teeny-Tiny Monkey. "All right," said the crocodile, "but please don't throw those things at me." So, Father Monkey swam to the other side and joined Teeny-Tiny Monkey and Mother Monkey up the tree.

And then, a strange thing happened. The crocodile began to cry. Big crocodile tears ran down his face. "It's very hard being a crocodile," he said. "Nobody likes me."

"We'll be your friends," said Teeny-Tiny Monkey, "if you promise not to eat us."

"I promise," said the crocodile, drying his tears.

From that day on, the crocodile kept his promise. The monkey family was very happy. They spent their days climbing up the trees and swinging through the branches, scratching where it itched the most, taking a nap in the middle of the day when it was very hot and picking the sweetest fruit and eating it all up.

"Mmmm … lovely."

And I don't know if this is true, but some people say that every now and then they see something very strange in the river, something they have never seen before; a crocodile swimming across the river with three monkeys riding on his back.

The End.

The context

Find Borneo on a map and talk about the climate, the vegetation, the mangrove trees and fruits and the animals that live there. This will help the children to understand the theme of the rhymes and the story.

Ways of telling

Vary the tone of your voice

Use different voices for the animals, a soft voice for Teeny-Tiny Monkey, a louder voice for Mother Monkey and so on. Create different voices for the angry crocodile and the sad crocodile.

Use actions

Mime different aspects of the story; for example, swimming fast across the river (use your arms), eating the delicious fruit and throwing the fruit at the crocodile.

Use props

If you can, show the children a mango and then enjoy eating it together. What does it taste like?

Early literacy

'Rhyme, rhythm and repetition'

The story has repeated elements that are important for getting the meaning across: for example, *Your teeth are ferocious; Stuff and nonsense; What are you doing in my river* – these repeated phrases will help the children to remember the language and structure of the story and are particularly valuable for children who are new to learning English. Encourage the children to learn these phrases and to join in with you.

Discuss the vocabulary

There might be words or phrases that the children will not have heard before – ferocious, stuff and nonsense, so give the children an opportunity to ask about these. Use the context of the story to help them to guess what a new word or phrase means.

Re-present the story

Invite the children to illustrate their favourite part of the story or make models of different characters. Display these creations and invite children to suggest captions or speech bubbles from the story that you can read together.

Playful maths

Discuss the terms teeny-tiny, medium-sized and bigger. Use examples of objects in the indoor or outdoor environment to illustrate the concepts. Bring in fruit of different sizes to compare (e.g. *raspberry, apple* and *grapefruit*).

The ending

Rhyme 1 and the story both end with a crocodile who is made to feel better. You could ask: Do you like the ending? What other endings can you think of? What would you say to the crocodile? Would you like him to be your friend?

Link to a published book

Dinnertime by Jan Pieńkowski

The theme of eating and being eaten is shown dramatically in this colourful, pop-up book, published in 1980. The book was engineered by Ted Smart. It is a cumulative story, where the frog eats flies, the vulture eats the frog, the gorilla eats the vulture, the tiger eats the gorilla and, naturally, the crocodile eats the tiger. But who eats the crocodile?

5 Hungry little mice

DOI: 10.4324/9781003358633-10

Rhymes and stories in this chapter

- Rhyme 1: Tippy tippy tip-toe
- Rhyme 2: Mrs. Mouse finds a house
- Rhyme 3 for the very young: Three blind mice
- Rhyme 4 for the very young: Pussy cat, pussy cat, where have you been?
- Rhyme 5 for the very young: Hickory dickory dock
- Story: George the Town Mouse and Henry the Country Mouse

Overarching themes

- New friendships

- Celebrating diversity

- Hospitality and welcome

Glossary

blind – unable to see
delicious – something that tastes wonderful
exotic – something new and different, often coming from a foreign country
footpath – a path you can walk along in the countryside, where cars are not allowed to go
frantic – hurrying around, feeling worried and anxious
gigantic – huge, enormous
moss – a small green plant that grows near water
skirting board – a strip of wood running along the bottom of a wall inside a room
stile – steps made of wood or stone so that you can climb to get into another field
theatre – a building where you can see plays or pantomimes
traffic – a lot of cars, buses or lorries moving along the road

RHYMES

Introduce the main theme

Talk about mice and invite the children to tell you what they know about them – their size, their colour, what they look like and so on. Ask the children to tell you their own mouse stories. Do any of the children have pet mice? Is anybody in their family frightened of mice?

You might want to take this opportunity to learn more about mice, perhaps by using information books or the Internet to find out more. How many kinds of mice are there in the UK? Where do they live? What do they eat? Older or more confident children could do their own research about mice and do a presentation for the class or for an assembly.

Rhyme 1

Tippy tippy tip-toe

Tippy tippy, tippy tippy,
Tippy tippy, tip-toe,
See the hungry little mice,
Running in the snow, snow.

Tippy tippy, tippy tippy,
Tippy tippy, tip-toe,
They couldn't find a thing to eat,
And so they had to go, go.

Rhyme 2

Mrs Mouse finds a house

Mrs Mouse was feeling sad,
Her egg-cup house was far too small.
She had to keep her tail tucked in
And curl up in a tiny ball.
So ...
She decided to move house.
But where could she go?

At last she found a big red slipper. But ...

Mrs Mouse was feeling sad,
Her slipper house was too gigantic,
It was such a long way from heel to toe,
And all this made her rather frantic.
So ...
She decided to move house.
But where could she go?

At last she found an old jam jar. Now ...

Mrs Mouse was feeling glad,
Her jam jar was exactly right,

Not too small and not too big,
Not too loose and not too tight.
So …
Wrapped up in her soft warm blanket,
She settled down and slept all night.
Sweet dreams.

Enjoy the rhymes together

Rhyme 1: Tippy tippy tip-toe

Talk about these two hungry mice who couldn't find anything to eat. Why was it difficult for them to find their food? Where could they go to find something to eat? Listen to the children's suggestions and create your own mouse story from what they say.

Chant the rhyme aloud, over and over again. Make mouth shapes as you say "Tippy, tippy, tippy, tippy". Respond to the child's attempts to imitate you as you open and close your mouth.

Use body gestures to bring the rhyme to life. For example, make two fingers run down your arm to represent the mice running in the snow. Similarly, when you say, "They couldn't find a thing to eat, And so they had to go, go", run your fingers softly up your right arm from your wrist to your shoulder. Encourage the children to make these movements and to join in with the chant. Use finger puppet mice to act out the rhyme as you say it.

Early literacy

Rhyme, rhythm and repetition

Play with the language and emphasise the alliterative "t" sounds as you say "Tippy, tippy, tippy, toe" and clap the rhythm as you recite the first two lines.

Move to the rhyme with the children. For example, tip-toe around looking eagerly left to right as you say the poem. Create a sense of urgency with swift, expectant movements.

Phonological awareness

Choose rhyming patterns: for example, *see* and *bee*; *tip, dip, lip, nip* and *rip*; and *snow, bow, low, mow, grow, row, sow* and *throw*. Make lists of patterned words and invented words and say these aloud with the children, pointing to the digraphs.

Point out the digraph "sn" in the word "snow" and make a list of other words beginning with "sn", for example *snake, snow, snooker* and *snatch*. Some children might enjoy making up alliterative "sn" or other digraph sentences, for example the sneaky snake in the snow snapped the snooker cue.

Left to right sequencing

Use the whiteboard to display the rhyme and engage in shared reading. You could have a little paper mouse on a stick to point to the words as you read them. The little mouse could run from left to right across the words as you say them and then go back to the beginning of the next line.

Role play

If you have enough space, encourage the children to enact the rhyme. They could show they are hungry by rubbing their tummies, and then they could run softly on tip-toe, before slowly disappearing into a nominated space (perhaps a corner of the room).

Rhyme 2: Mrs Mouse finds a house

As you chant this rhyme, use your facial expressions to indicate Mrs Mouse feeling sad and glad. Use your hands to show how small the egg-cup is, how big the slipper is and how the jam jar is "exactly right". Pause dramatically as you chant "So" and "But" and "And now". You could show the children an egg-cup, a (rather large) slipper and a jam jar to indicate size difference and to help the children understand the concepts of "big", "small" and "exactly right".

Early literacy

Rhyme, rhythm and repetition

Emphasise the pairs of rhyming words throughout: small – ball; gigantic – frantic; right – tight. Pause to encourage the children to guess the second word in the rhyming pair.

Play with the language

Talk about the rhyme in Mouse and House. Think of other animals and try to find a rhyming word to match the animal with its house. For example, Mr Snail lived in a pail; Mrs Cat lived in a flat. Ask the children for ideas and share these together.

Phonological awareness

Draw attention to the patterning of three-letter consonant-vowel-consonant words that occur throughout (*sad, cup, big, red, but* and *jam*) and make lists of similar words. Provide letter pieces or magnetic letters and encourage children to make lists of three-letter consonant-vowel-consonant words.

Role play

If you have room, chant the rhyme while the children each stand in a space. They can curl up small in their egg-cup, then pretend to be in a huge slipper until they finally settle down to sleep in their jam jar.

Playful maths

Put some small mouse figures in the sand or other snow-like substance. Join in with the children's small world play to model appropriate mathematical vocabulary. Count the mice. Make up games to encourage mathematical thinking. "Oh no!" The little mouse cannot run so fast! How many mice got to the end. How many more are still running?

Use outdoor spaces

Make a mouse course, with tunnels and obstacles for children to navigate as they move towards the finishing line. Encourage the mice to take turns and be careful not to run into each other. The children could make mouse certificates or medals.

Ideas to support very young children

Rhyme 3

Three blind mice
Three blind mice,
Three blind mice,
See how they run,
See how they run.
They all ran after the farmer's wife
Who cut off their tails with a carving knife.
Did ever you see such a thing in your life
As three blind mice?

Rhyme 4

Pussy cat, pussy cat, where have you been?
Pussy cat, pussy cat, where have you been?
I've been up to London to visit the queen.
Pussy cat, pussy cat, what did you there?
I frightened a little mouse under her chair.

Rhyme 5

Hickory dickory dock
Hickory, dickory, dock!
The mouse ran up the clock!
The clock struck one,
The mouse ran down!
Hickory, dickory, dock!

Ways of telling

Use facial expressions and mime to enact these rhymes and always encourage the children to join in. There are well-known tunes for Three Blind Mice, Hickory Dickory Dock and Pussy Cat, Pussy Cat. Sing these rhymes for the children so they can listen and learn to join in.

Use three fingers to count the mice in "Three Blind Mice." Cover your hands over your eyes to show that the mice can't see and move your index finger and middle finger quickly up your arm to "see how they run." Mime chopping off their tails and encourage the children to join in with all these movements. Ask: "Did you ever see such a thing in your life?" very expressively, moving your head slowly from side to side, as though in disbelief.

When you chant "Hickory dickory dock," clasp your hands together and sway your arms from side to side to indicate the ticking of the clock. Hold up one finger to show "the clock struck one" and move your index finger and third finger quickly down your arm to show "the mouse ran down!" Use your eyes to create a sense of suspense and danger.

Phonological awareness

Take the opportunity to reinforce the *ch* digraph in Pussy Cat, Pussy Cat. Point to the *ch* in *chair* and ask the children to think of other words beginning with this sound (e.g. *church, children, chop* and *chips*). Begin a *ch* shopping list, for example *chips, chocolate, cheese*, and encourage the children to add to it.

Using the word *chair* again, concentrate on the *air* ending and think of other words that use this spelling pattern (e.g. *hair, fair* and *pair*)

Re-present the rhymes

Give each child a paper plate and invite them to draw or paint their favourite foods on the plate. Share everyone's choices with the group and display the plates for everyone to see.

STORY: GEORGE THE TOWN MOUSE AND HENRY THE COUNTRY MOUSE

There was once a mouse called George. He lived in a tiny room under the skirting board of a big house in the middle of London town. There was a lot of traffic outside and sometimes George could hear noisy planes going over the house, but his room was very comfortable; it had a little table and a chair, a soft bed and some bookshelves filled with his favourite books. George had plenty to eat too. When the family who lived in the house had gone to bed, George tip-toed into the kitchen and if he was lucky he found bits of pizza, a few chips and some cheese, and sometimes there was leftover trifle, chocolate cake and jelly. So all in all, it was a good place to live.

One morning George woke up, rubbed his eyes and thought, "What shall I do today? I know. I'll visit cousin Henry. We haven't seen each other for ages." And so, George put on his best coat and hat and off he went. Henry lived in the country, a long way from the noise of London town.

George knew the way. He went under the front door, across the busy road, alongside the shops, through the market, past the theatre and down the alleyway. At last, he left the town behind. "Here's the footpath," he said. "I just need to go past the cows, over the stile, round the pond, and then I'm there!" George tried to sound brave, but he was really a little bit frightened.

"I hope the cows don't tread on me!" he thought, as he tip-toed round their feet.

"I hope I don't fall in the pond!" he thought, as he picked his way round the edge of the water.

"I hope I don't hurt myself when I cross the stile!" he thought, as he lifted himself over the wooden posts.

Then, he stopped and listened. "What's that noise?" he thought. The cows were mooing, the birds were singing and the bees were buzzing. It was all rather strange … but on he went and at last he reached Henry's door.

"Hello, George!" said Henry. "Come on in." Henry lived in an old rabbit hole. He'd lined it with straw to make it cosy. His little bed was stuffed with feathers, and he had filled his sofa with moss. George wasn't used to living in the country. "I'm not sure I'm going to like it here," he thought, "but I don't want to hurt Henry's feelings. After all, I'm only going to stay for one night and then I'll be back home in my own little room."

"Sit down after your long journey," said Henry, "and I'll make us a pot of tea." Henry poured the tea into the cups. George took a sip and pulled a face. "What's this?"

he said. "Tea," said Henry. "That's not tea!" said George. "Yes, it is," said Henry. "It's made with dandelions. I love it." "Well I don't," said George. "Never mind," said Henry. "Let's have something to eat." George wondered what Henry was going to bring him, and when he saw his plate of food, he could hardly believe his eyes. This wasn't what he called food! There were four hazel nuts, six peas, two tiny carrots, three dandelion leaves and a lettuce leaf. "I collected all these specially for you," said Henry, proudly. "I hope you like them." George tried to smile, and he said "Thank you" very politely because he knew that Henry had gone to a lot of trouble and he didn't want to hurt his feelings, but oh, how he wished he had some pizza and chips, and trifle and jelly and ice cream. George munched his way sadly through the four hazel nuts, six peas, two tiny carrots, three dandelion leaves and the lettuce leaf. Then, it was time for bed. He curled up on the old feather bed, still feeling very hungry. Then, he began to sneeze. "It must be the feathers," he thought. Finally, he dropped off to sleep.

In the morning, he had an idea. "I tell you what," he said to Henry, "Why don't you come back to London with me and I'll show you around my house." "I'd love to," said Henry, and so Henry packed a little bag. He closed his door, and they started out for London town.

They went round the pond, over the stile, past the cows and along the footpath until they saw lots of houses and shops and factories. Henry was frightened. The lorries thundered past him on the road, and the noise from the huge planes over his head made him cover his ears. Lots of times, he thought he was going to be trampled to death by all the people on the pavement. "It's so big and noisy," he said. "Don't be frightened," said George. "That's my house over there. Not far now."

Henry followed George down the alleyway, past the theatre, through the market, across the busy road, under the front door and into the gap in the skirting board. "Phew!" said Henry. "I didn't think I'd be brave enough to do that!" "We're both brave," said George. "I didn't think I'd be able to go past all those cows, but I did it."

George took Henry into his tiny room. "Now," he said, "when the family's gone to bed we'll have a feast!" And that's what they did. They ate up all the leftovers from supper – tonight it was chop suey, chow mein, cheddar cheese, chutney and chocolate mousse. "Mmmm," said Henry. "I've never had such delicious food!" "I thought you'd like it!" said George.

But that night, Henry had terrible pains in his stomach. "All your lovely food is a little bit too exotic for me," he said to George in the morning. "I think perhaps I should get back to my own little house."

"I understand," said George. "It's the same for both of us. I don't think I could ever get used to the things you eat. Never mind! I'll take you home as far as the stile so you don't get lost."

"Thank you," said Henry. So, George took Henry back through the streets of London and into the countryside until they got as far as the stile and he could see his rabbit hole. "Good-bye," said George. "Good-bye," said Henry. But just before he left, Henry said, "I've got an idea. Next time we meet why don't we both bring a picnic and meet by the pond. Then we can have a good talk and eat our own food."

And that's exactly what they did.

Ways of telling

If you are going to tell the story from memory, try to learn the sequence of events and use your own words to describe George and Henry's journeys. Put lots of conversation into your re-telling, and, if you like, invent special voices for George and Henry.

Re-present the story

Invite the children to draw or paint the mice in the story. Ask the children what it might feel like to be a little mouse living in a town. How would such a tiny animal cross the road safely? Would the town be quiet or noisy? Would the mouse be afraid? Would it be safer or more frightening to live in the country? Children might also like to build models of the two dwellings. Encourage children to talk about their creations.

When you have shared the story, create a story map with the children, showing how George got from his own room to Henry's house, and how they both came back to London town again. Use the places from the story: *the front door, the busy road, the shops, the market, the theatre and the alleyway, the stile, the pond.* Ask the children to draw these places and suggest captions at points of interest (e.g. *This is George's house. This is where the cows frightened George. This is where George and Henry had their picnic.*) Ask older children to make their own story map of their journey to school or nursery.

Early literacy

Discuss the vocabulary

Introduce unfamiliar vocabulary. There are some words and phrases in the story that the children might not have met before. Ask them to listen out for these words or draw their attention to some of these examples: *skirting board, traffic, theatre, footpath, stile, moss, dandelions, delicious* and *exotic.*

Draw attention to the use of prepositions. Emphasise particular prepositions as you read or tell the story: *under, across, along/alongside, through, past, over, round* and *down.* Encourage the children to use a variety of propositions in their own retellings. Read other stories where prepositions are used in an interesting way; for example,

We're Going on a Bear Hunt (Michael Rosen and Helen Oxenbury) and Rosie's Walk (Pat Hutchins).

Encourage writing

Show the children how to make a list. For example, make lists of all the different kinds of food George and Henry like to eat. Invite the children to write their own lists of their favourite foods.

Role play

Hot seat yourself as George or Henry and invite the children to ask you questions about your life. If you have room, you could enact George and Henry's journeys. Two children could be the mice; a group could pose as large buildings, cows or trees; and the mice children could make their way through the obstacles.

Link to a published book

A Dark, Dark Tale by Ruth Brown

A Dark Dark Tale enacts a journey through a dark wood and into a dark house. It follows a cat up the steep staircase into a room with a toy cupboard which contains a little box. In the tiny box, there is a tiny chest, table, rug and a bed. And who should be sleeping in the bed but a tiny mouse. Children will enjoy looking at the mouse's room which is probably similar to George's cosy room.

6 Wind and sun

DOI: 10.4324/9781003358633-11

Rhymes and stories in this chapter

- Rhyme 1: The north wind doth blow
- Rhyme 2: Whether the weather be fine
- Rhyme 3 for the very young: I hear raindrops
- Story: The north wind and the sun

Overarching themes

- Caring for the environment
- Building shelters from the environment
- Protecting wildlife
- Talking about seasonal and daily weather patterns

Glossary

barn – a building on a farm where animals are kept or where hay or straw is stored

doth – an old-fashioned way of saying "does." We sometimes read the word "doth" in rhymes and stories from long ago

hark – an old-fashioned way of saying "listen"

RHYMES

Introduce the main theme

Talk to the children about the kinds of weather they like and don't like and the sorts of clothes they wear at different times of the year. (You could make a useful link here with Rhyme and Story No. 1 – **Boots and Shoes**.) Young children are probably not conscious of weather patterns in the way that adults are, but they do know if it is hot or cold, and of course they are constantly being told by parents or teachers that they can play outdoors as long as they put their coats on.

Rhyme 1

The north wind doth blow
The north wind doth blow,
And we shall have snow
And what will the robin do then,

Poor thing?
He'll sit in a barn,
And keep himself warm,
And hide his head under his wing,
Poor thing.

Rhyme 2

Whether the weather be fine
Whether the weather be fine
Or whether the weather be not
We'll weather the weather
Whatever the weather
Whether we like it or not

Enjoy the rhymes together

Go outside with the children. Experience the weather together and talk about it.

Make up actions to match Rhyme 1. Learn the rhyme and chant it over and over again. Use actions and encourage the children to join in:

- *The north wind doth blow* – puff your cheeks out and breathe out, making a whooshing sound as you do so.
- *And we shall have snow* – look up at the ceiling, put your arms above your head and wiggle your fingers downwards. Clasp your arms together and shiver with cold.
- *And what will the robin do then, Poor thing?* Open up your arms as you question what the robin will do. Make a sad, worried face. Point to the picture of the robin and shake your head.
- *He'll sit in a barn and keep himself warm* – wrap your arms around yourself.
- *And hide his head under his wing* – put your head under your arm.

Recite Rhyme 2 before you go outside with the children. Talk about appropriate clothing and protection in different weather conditions. Enjoy the humour and rhythm of the rhyme.

Early literacy

Writing

Write the words to "The North Wind Doth Blow" and "Whether the weather be fine" on a whiteboard or on card, so the children can see the words as you read the rhymes.

Provide clipboards and writing materials in different areas, outdoors and indoors. Encourage the children to watch the birds, both at home and in your school or nursery setting and make lists of the different species they see. Ask them to draw or paint the birds and display their artwork.

Phonological awareness

Look closely at the ending *ing*: *wing/thing* in "The North Wind Doth Blow" and make a list of other words with this common ending. Read them together.

Look at the *ow* digraph in *snow/blow* and ask the children to give you examples of other words or made-up words ending in this digraph, for example *mow, row, sow* or *low*. Some children might suggest words like *how* and *now*. If they do this, use the opportunity to explain the differences in pronunciation.

Play with language

Rhyme 2 is a play on words. Talk about words that sound the same but have different meanings, for example count (as in counting numbers) and Count (as in an important person) or train (as in a vehicle with an engine) and train (as in a personal trainer).

Draw attention to the homophones in "whether" and "weather". Explain that "whether" and "weather" are pronounced in the same way but that they have different meanings. In this rhyme, "Whether" is used to mean "if" or "even if" (so, e.g. We're going out *even if* it's cold; We're going out *whether* it's cold or hot). Talk about the phrase: "whether the weather".

Another use of "weather" is as a verb meaning we will stand firm and not be defeated. Ask the children if they have ever "weathered the weather" and what their experience was.

Explore the word "doth". Explain that "doth" is an old word meaning "does" and we sometimes find this word in rhymes and stories from long ago.

Playful maths

Invite children to sequence daily routines and days of the week. They could try to match the days with different weather symbols. Help children to develop mathematical fluency. Use language such as *before* and *after, next, first, today, yesterday, tomorrow, morning, afternoon* and *evening* within your conversations and as you talk about your daily routines. "Yesterday it was rainy. It is sunny this morning. I wonder if it will still be sunny this afternoon."

Ideas to inspire very young children

Rhyme 3

I hear raindrops
I hear raindrops.
I hear raindrops.
Hark, don't you?
Hark, don't you?
Pitter, patter raindrops!
Pitter, patter raindrops!
I'm wet through.
So are you.

Enjoy the rhyme together

Encourage the children to join in with you as you sing this rhyme. Use actions to bring the rhyme to life:

■ I hear raindrops.
  Cup your hands behind your ears to indicate that you are listening.

■ Hark, don't you?
  Point to one of the children and encourage them to point to one another.

■ Pitter, patter raindrops!
  Wiggle your fingers in a downward motion.

■ I'm wet through.
  Shake the water off yourself.
  So are you.
  Look with surprise at someone.

Plan opportunities for very young children to experience different weather conditions. Create an outdoor sleeping area where babies can experience being outdoors, and where they can smell the smells, breathe the air and feel the different temperatures.

Organise for children to have easily accessible outdoor clothing and footwear so that very young children can choose to go outdoors when they want to play in the snow and rain and be protected in cold and wet weather.

Stimulate talk

Talk about windy and snowy weather. Invite the children to tell you stories about when they have been out in the wind or the snow.

Talk about birds in the winter. Why is it difficult for birds to keep warm in cold weather? How can we help them? Invite children to tell you their own stories about feeding the birds or perhaps going bird-watching with their families.

Re-present their own weather experiences

Ask the children to draw a picture or act out a mime to illustrate their own experiences of being out in different weathers. Suggest movements to match their ideas, for example draw your shoulders if they talk about feeling cold. Help them to write a caption to accompany their pictures and actions.

Foster a love of nature

Make a feeding station for the birds and set it up near your classroom. Use information books or the Internet to research the different birds you see and the kinds of food you should put out for them. Older children can write to the Royal Society for the Protection of Birds (RSPB) or the British Trust for Ornithology (BTO) for more information:

RSPB, The Lodge, Sandy, SG19 2DL

BTO, The Nunnery, Thetford, Norfolk, IP24 2PU.

STORY: THE NORTH WIND AND THE SUN

One day, the North Wind and the Sun met each other high up in the sky.

"Good morning, Sun," said the North Wind.

"Good morning, North Wind," said the Sun. "What are you going to do today?"

"Well, I thought I'd blow and blow with all my strength so that the trees bend, the children's hats get blown off and the butterflies get tossed around in the sky! Should be fun!"

"That sounds very mean to me," said the Sun. "I sometimes think you're a bit of a bully. Why can't you be gentle and kind?"

"It's only a game!" said the North Wind. "Talking of games, why don't we have a competition? You see that man down there, the one wearing the long coat?"

The Sun peered down. "Yes, I can see him. It's Mr. Jones. He takes his dog for a walk across that field every day."

"Well," said the North Wind. "Let's see which one of us can get him to take his coat off!"

"Very well," said the Sun. "You go first."

The North Wind puffed out his cheeks and he blew and blew and blew. He blew so hard that the trees were bent almost double, the little birds hid in their nests and the children ran inside to get out of the wind, holding their hats on their heads. But Mr. Jones just wrapped his coat more tightly around him and fastened his belt so that his coat did not blow off. The North Wind blew even harder – he blew and blew and blew, but Mr. Jones turned his back to the wind and hurried home across the field with his little dog.

"My turn now," said the Sun. The Sun came out from behind some clouds and shone down on the field. Mr. Jones looked up into the sky. "Ah, at last the sun has come out!" he said to his dog. "Thank goodness that awful wind has stopped blowing and now it's a bit warmer." Mr. Jones began to feel so warm that he undid the top button of his coat. The Sun shone down even more strongly.

"Phew, it's really getting hot now!" said Mr. Jones, and he undid the rest of the buttons on his coat. The Sun shone down even more strongly.

"Phew," said Mr. Jones. He wiped his forehead. "I shall have to take my coat off." And this is just what he did.

Then, the Sun turned to the North Wind, who was looking rather cross. "I've won," said the Sun. "I don't know why," said the North Wind in a grumpy voice. "I'm stronger than you."

"You may be stronger than me," said the Sun, "but I'm much more gentle than you are, and that's why Mr. Jones took his coat off." The North Wind nodded his head. "I've never thought about that," he said. "Perhaps you're right. I'll try and be more like you in the future." The North Wind and the Sun shook hands.

"Good-bye, Sun," said the North Wind.

"Good-bye, North Wind," said the Sun. "See you tomorrow."

Ways of telling

As you tell the story, mime the actions of the North Wind, puffing out your cheeks and blowing hard. Raise your arms slowly and gently to show the Sun warming the earth below. Show how Mr. Jones wraps his coat tightly round him and fastens his belt against the wind. Invite the children to copy these actions. If you like, you can create different voices for the North Wind and the Sun.

Early literacy

Writing

Invite the children to write their own story of The North Wind and the Sun. Help them use the different keys of the computer if they choose to write their stories in this way.

Reading labels

Invite the children to update the chart every day, using particular words written on strips of card (e.g. *Today it is … hot, sunny, cold, snowy, windy, icy, foggy, rainy.*). Read the sentence together every day.

Playful maths

Use comparative language within children's play to help them build up their mathematical fluency, for example *greater than, larger than* or *smaller than*. Talk about the strength of the wind and how it can knock things down with its force. Help children to name, describe, compare and sort different everyday objects or familiar story characters according to strength. They could make a strong and weak set, for example, a giant and hammer in one set, and a fairy and feather in another. Encourage children to suggest other categories for sorting.

Encourage creativity

Re-present the story

Ask the children to draw or paint their favourite part of the story. Share their work with the class and display their illustrations to talk about with their families and carers.

Role play

In groups of five, each child plays a character from the story and one tells the story (Mr. Jones, the dog, the North Wind, The Sun and the Narrator). Give the children time to practise their play before they enact it for the other children or perhaps for the whole school in an assembly.

Link to a published book

One snowy night by Nick Butterworth

This is a cumulative story about a man who takes in more and more animals to shelter them from the snow storm. They all keep each other awake in Percy's bed until finally they decide to find other places to sleep in the cottage. Percy finally settles to sleep in his bed with his friends snuggled in drawers and on top of cupboards.

7 Precious toys and playthings

DOI: 10.4324/9781003358633-12

Rhymes and stories in this chapter

- Rhyme 1: Miss Polly had a dolly
- Rhyme 2: Five little cuddly dolls
- Rhyme 3 for the very young: Teddy bear teddy bear
- Story: The girl who gave her precious doll away – A Comanche story

Overarching themes

- Giving things away to support others

- Working together for a common purpose

- Being kind and generous

Glossary

ashes – grey dust that remains after the fire
bill – a note about how much something costs
carve – cut and scrape something carefully to make a new shape
dwindling – something that is getting smaller or dying, like a fire
famine – when there is not enough food to feed the people, so they become sick
shaman – a holy person, like a priest, guru, rabbi or imam

RHYMES

Introduce the main theme

Young children love to play with dolls, action toys or other special, cuddly toys. Make a collection of different dolls, soft toys and action people for children to play with and talk about. Invite children to bring in their own special ones from home to show their friends. Designate a special area for these toys with name labels.

Talk about the materials of different dolls, for example cloth, plastic, wood and rubber. Invite children to paint pictures of their favourite dolls. Find an old-fashioned doll and other old-fashioned doll accessories, if possible, to show to children and invite them to talk about how they differ to current dolls. Perhaps you could bring alongside your doll or teddy bear too.

Rhyme 1

Miss Polly

Miss Polly had a dolly who was sick, sick, sick,
So she called for the doctor to be quick, quick, quick.
The doctor came with his bag and his hat
And he knocked on the door with a rat–a–tat–tat.

He looked at the dolly and he shook his head,
And he said: "Miss Polly put her straight to bed!"
He wrote on a paper for a pill, pill, pill.
"I'll be back in the morning with my bill, bill, bill."

Enjoy the rhyme together

Enjoy reciting the rhyme or singing it with the children. Use actions to match the words as you sing them. For example, you could mime rocking the doll, knocking on the door and waving goodbye. Invite children to hold their doll as they chant the rhyme with you.

Talk about Miss Polly and her dolly. What happens in the rhyme? Ask the children what happens to them when they get sick. Do they go to the doctor? Do they like going to the doctor? Do they have to take any medicine? What sorts of medicine do they take? What about injections?

Allow different children to be Miss Polly and the Doctor as you sing the song. They can then choose different children to take over the roles.

Role play

Suggest to the children that they set up a doll's hospital. Provide bandages, clipboards, labels and other play materials to encourage purposeful writing, build friendships and use talk as part of their play. Participate in children's play to extend their vocabulary.

Make props with children as they engage with different aspects of the play. For example, a child may remember going to hospital and getting a certificate after having a particular treatment. Make nurse's badges and children's certificates with the children. Build up the play over a period of time based on children's experiences.

Re-present the rhymes

Invite children to paint pictures or make collages of their favourite doll, soft toy or action toy. Provide a range of fabrics and materials for them to create their images. Talk about the materials they choose. Model descriptive language to help children talk about things and support their language development, for example *soft, rough, shiny, thick* and *pale*.

Early literacy

Phonological awareness

Write the rhyme on a large piece of paper or whiteboard so that the children can see the words. As you read the rhyme, emphasise the rhyming sounds and the repeated words in the text: *pill, pill, pill and bill, bill, bill*. Pause just before the rhyming word so the children can anticipate and join in. Encourage children suggest other words that rhyme, for example *fill, till, mill, will*, or invent nonsense-words, for example *noo, noo, noo*. Be playful with language.

Draw attention to the sounds and patterns of the poem. Look closely at the spelling patterns: *sick, quick, hat, tat, head, bed, pill, bill*, pointing out the initial sound(s), the phonic patterns and the word endings.

Left to right sequencing

Use an enlarged copy of the rhyme and run your finger along each line to demonstrate left-to-right sequencing. Invite the children to sequence the rhyme using picture cards, toys or small world objects.

Playful maths

- Make up number songs and games about dolls, for example:

Rhyme 2

> *Five little cuddly dolls...*
> Five little cuddly dolls on Samantha's bed,
> all snuggled up with blankets on the top,
> along came Abdullah with a buggy one day,
> he held a cuddly doll and took it out to play.
> Four cuddly dolls etc...

- Post maths challenges about dolls, soft toys or action toys, for example.
  There are five dolls in the pram. My friend takes one out to give them tea. How many are left on in the pram?

- Play sorting games with the toys. Ask children to sort the dolls, soft toys and action toys according to different criteria, for example materials, type or size.
  Sort the dolls in order of size, from smallest to biggest.

- Make a toy shop. Invite children to suggest prices for the toys. Encourage children to name and write numbers and count coins as part of their play.

Ideas to inspire very young children

Rhyme 3

Teddy bear teddy bear
Teddy bear, teddy bear, turn around.
Teddy bear, teddy bear, touch the ground.
Teddy bear, teddy bear, reach up high.
Teddy bear, teddy bear, touch the sky.
Teddy bear, teddy bear, bend down low.
Teddy bear, teddy bear, touch your toes!
Teddy bear, teddy bear, turn out the light
Teddy bear, teddy bear, say Goodnight.

Sing this action-song and other playful songs with children as you hold them and move around the learning space. Respond to children's reactions as you sing and move. Invent other actions, for example climb a tree or open the door.

If the child appears to enjoy a particular part of the song, develop this part and repeat it. Babies and very young children love repetition.

Foster a love of nature

Use outdoor spaces to sing rhymes and make big movements as you sing. Organise a doll's or teddy bear's picnic outdoors. Invite the children to write a shopping list for the picnic and plan what they need to put in the picnic basket. Help the children make a poster to announce the picnic with directions of how to get to the picnic spot.

Invite children to talk about what they see and hear in the outdoor environment as part of the picnic activities.

STORY: THE GIRL WHO GAVE HER PRECIOUS DOLL AWAY – A COMANCHE STORY

Once upon a time, there was a girl called Topsannah who had a lovely doll. Her grandfather carved the doll out of wood. Her mother made the dress. Her grandmother squashed berries to make dye and paint the eyes and mouth. Her father ground a stone to make a shiny belt.

Topsannah had another name too. The people who looked after her in the village called her Topsannah-the-girl-who-is-on-her-own. This was because her mother, father, grandmother and grandfather had all died in a terrible famine. The people of the village looked after her, but she still missed her family. Topsannah-the girl-who-is-on-her-own loved her doll very much because it reminded her of her grandparents and her mother and father.

The famine had come to the village because there had been no rain for three years. The land where she lived had become very dry, and the people could no longer grow enough food to feed everyone. There was no wheat to make bread, no apples on the trees, no vegetables and no milk or cheese because the goats and cattle were too thin to make any milk. Many people died of hunger, including Topsannah's family.

The people of the village were worried. They met together every week to talk about what they could do to make things better. How could they make it rain? How could they grow their crops again? How could they feed their babies? But no answers came.

One day the shaman, or holy man, came to the meeting very excited. He had heard a message from God to the people. He said: "We have become very selfish. We have taken the plants and trees of the earth to feed ourselves and make the things we want. But we have not given anything back to the earth. Now we must give our most precious possession back to the earth. Then the rain will return and the plants and trees will grow again and we will live."

The people of the village discussed what they could give. What was the most precious thing they could give? One lady wondered: "Should I give the blanket that keeps me warm at night?" Another asked: "Should I give my cooking pot that I use to cook food for my family? But is it precious now there is nothing to cook?" A farmer asked: "Is my spade the most precious thing? Perhaps it used to be, but the ground is too hard to dig now, so is it still precious?" Another questioned: "Should I give our rug that we sit on in our tent, even though it's nearly worn out?" They made suggestions until late in the night but could not agree on what to give.

But all this time, Topsannah-the-girl-who-is-on-her-own had been listening to what the people said. When everyone went back to their tents to rest, Topsannah-the-girl-on-her-own stayed by the fire and thought about her doll. Her doll was her most precious possession. She knew she must give it, but she did not want to. She held her doll for a long time and stroked her hair.

When everyone else was asleep, she put her doll gently on the dwindling fire and watched it burn slowly until only ashes and a few bits of the doll were left.

When the ashes were cool, just before morning, Topsannah-the girl-on-her-own took a handful of the ashes and sprinkled it all around, then she went to bed and fell asleep.

She was awakened by the sound of rain and people crying out: "God is good!" "God has sent us rain!" "God has saved us!"

All around the village, Topsannah-the-girl-who-is-on-her-own saw hundreds and thousands of little blue flowers everywhere. They were little wild lupins that had come up in the rain. It was a wonderful sight!

The villagers found the remains of the girl's doll in the ashes and understood what had happened. Topsannah-the-girl-who-is-on-her-own had given her most precious possession, her doll. From then on, she was given a new name: Topsannah-the-girl-who-saved-us.

Topsannah-the girl-who-saved-us lived happily ever after in the village. She had lots of friends. There was plenty of food for everyone, and the people were always kind to each other. From then on, they all thanked God for the good things of the earth, and were never hungry again.

Enjoy the story together

Discuss the context. Show children Texas on the map on the world or globe. Talk about the people who first inhabited that land.

Use visual images to encourage the children to respond. Invite children to sequence the story, using picture cards or props. If you can, dress a doll in Native American costume to show the children what Topsannah's doll might have looked like.

Ways of telling

Vary the tone of your voice

Use different voices to express emotions. Use a worried voice when the people are worried about their families or worried because they don't know what to offer up. Use a joyful voice when you tell the part about the flowers and the rain.

Vary the pace

Say the sad bits of the story more slowly with a sad face. Pause as the people wonder what to give up. Pause as the girl thinks about what she is about to do, burn her precious doll.

Use actions

Use different actions to enliven the story-telling. For example, when the women wonder what to give, make actions for cooking in the cooking pot or sleeping under the blanket. You could also use your hands to express a sense of helplessness or happiness. Open your hands out as you wonder what to do, or raise your hands in the air to show how happy you are.

Ask questions

Invite children to suggest other ideas of what they would give. Where do they think the girl could live after the rains? What happens to the girl after the rains come? Does she make another doll? Does she have a friend? What name would you give to the girl?

Role play

Create a small world scene of the story with the different people of the village, the shaman and the girl. Put other props in the small world scene to support understanding of the context. Join in children's play to build on their ideas and extend language.

Set up a role play with props or puppets for children to re-enact the story in their own words. Make a make-shift tent, provide rugs and a simple doll.

Set up a puppet area where children can act out the story to each other, with a home-made Comanche puppet.

Early literacy

Write lists

Provide writing materials in the story area for children to make lists of their most special things.

Introduce non-fiction publications

Provide information books and help children explore safe websites about the weather and climate. Talk about the importance of caring for the planet and the need for everyone to play their part.

Playful maths

Talk about big numbers children might have heard of, for example a hundred, a thousand or a million. Help children to estimate numbers. How many flowers in the flower bed? How many forks in the drawer? Can they count the hairs in their head or the grains of sand in the sand pit?

Set up a counting table with collections of things for children to count, number cards, rulers, counting sticks, calculators, number displays, etc. Find different opportunities in the day to count together and identify numbers. Provide writing materials for children to write numbers.

Encourage creativity

Invite the children to make their own special dolls. They could illustrate their favourite part of the rhyme and story to display in the story area.

Link to a published book

Dogger by Shirley Hughes

This classic, award winning picture book, published in 1977, is about a boy who loses his favourite toy, a soft dog called Dogger. The boy's family are very sympathetic with him and show him lots of affection. His sister lends him her favourite toy to help him go to sleep, but nothing seems to help. Finally, he is reunited with his toy. The story is about love and loss. Readers and children enjoy this book as much as each other.

8 Water for life

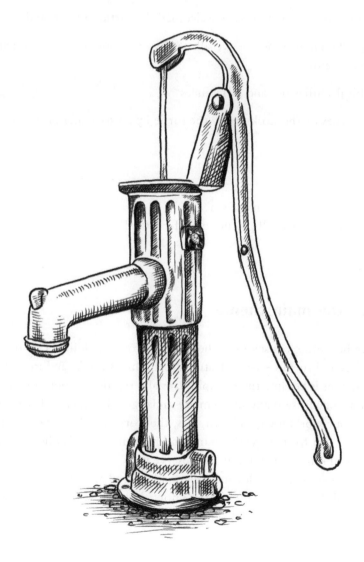

DOI: 10.4324/9781003358633-13

Rhymes and stories in this chapter

- Rhyme 1: What's that there?
- Rhyme 2 for the very young: Five little speckled frogs
- Story: The Flying Turtle – A story from India

Overarching themes

- Building friendship – the storks go out of their way to help the turtle

- Welcoming others – the monkeys welcomed the turtle to their land

- Caring for the environment – we all need to care for the environment to avoid droughts and famine

- Geographical similarities and differences

- Making journeys – the storks carry the turtle by air to a safer place

Glossary

foam – lots of tiny bubbles on the sea
speckled – with lots of small patches of different colours

RHYMES

Introduce the main theme

Children are becoming conscious of the need to protect wildlife. The animals in this chapter – frogs and turtles – often feature in children's books and in natural history programmes. This is because these amphibians and reptiles are not only interesting to observe but also because many of them are endangered, a theme that is increasingly significant in our world today. The rhymes, the story and the suggested activities in this chapter are fun to share with young children and will also help them to think about the animal kingdom and how to preserve it.

Show pictures of frogs, turtles and other endangered animals. If possible, organise a visit to a pond. Find out what children know about these creatures. Display books about frogs, turtles and other land and water creatures.

Rhyme 1

What's that there?

Shh ... Listen. What's that there?
It's a big white egg, and it's buried in the sand.
But who's inside? Shall we see?
It's a little baby turtle, trying to get free.
Push, push, push, push.

Shh ... Listen. What's that there?
It's a little baby turtle and he's climbing up the sand.
But who's that there? Shall we see?
It's a great big seagull sitting in a tree.
Quick, quick, quick, quick.

Shh ... Listen. What's that there?
It's the little baby turtle walking on the sand.
Where will he go? Shall we see?
The little baby turtle can smell the deep blue sea.
Plod, plod, plod, plod.

Shh ... Listen. What's that there?
It's the little baby turtle swimming in the foam.
Where will he go? Shall we see?
The little baby turtle has made it to his home!
Swim, swim, swim, swim.

Enjoy the rhyme together

Ask the children if they have seen baby turtles emerging from their nest in the sand and making their way to the sea, hoping the seagulls don't catch them. Chant the rhyme over and over again, inviting the children to join in.

Dramatise the rhyme

Verse 1

Put your finger to your lips when you say "Ssh" and cup your hands behind your ears as you whisper the word "listen". Point towards the floor as you ask "What's that there?" and gently hold your palms together to help the children to envisage the egg and the baby turtle emerging. Use your hands to show how the baby turtle pushes its way out of the egg.

Verse 2

Use the fingers of one hand against your other arm to indicate the baby turtle climbing up through the sand. Look up to envisage the seagull watching the turtle and increase the speed of your fingers as the baby turtle runs to the sea.

Verse 3

Raise your head to breathe in to smell the sea and then use your hands to show the baby turtle plodding on to the sea.

Verse 4

Use your hands and arms to show how the baby turtle uses its flippers to swim away from the shore.

Early literacy

Rhyme, rhythm and repetition

In addition to the gestures suggested above, chant each verse rhythmically, almost in a sing-song way, but with some drama added to your chanting. "Push, push, push, push" and "Plod, plod, plod, plod" can be rather slow, but speed up to for repeated "Quick, quick, quick, quick" and be more relaxed for "Swim, swim, swim, swim".

Play with the language

Encourage the children to join in with the words and actions of repeated phrases throughout.

Phonological awareness

The repeated words: *Push, plod, quick* and *swim* can be used to teach spelling patterns: consonant clusters ("pl" and "sw"); grapheme ("sh").

Role play

Take the children outdoors, if you can, and invite them to be baby turtles, curling up small in the egg, pushing their way out, climbing up through the sand, walking quickly along the beach and then swimming in the sea.

Suggest large and small movements and encourage children to make high and small shapes with their bodies.

Ideas to inspire very young children

Rhyme 2

Five little speckled frogs
Five little speckled frogs
Sat on a speckled log
Eating some most delicious worms – Mmm, Mmm.
One jumped into the pool
Where it was nice and cool
Then there were four speckled frogs – yes, yes!
Four little speckled frogs....

Sing the rhyme together, outdoors if possible. Draw a circle in chalk or use objects to represent the pond. Place a log, or some boxes, just outside the circle so that children can act out the rhyme, sitting on the speckled log and jumping into the pool.

In the summer, with appropriate adult supervision, you can use a real paddling pool so that children can experience the cool water.

Set up a small world area with counters to represent frogs and a pond environment to encourage children to re-enact the scene as part of their play. Join in with children's play, inserting vocabulary, as needed, and including other children in the game. Such playful and sensitive interventions will support children's social and communication development.

Playful maths

Ask the children to stand by the pond to represent the frogs and jump into the pool in turns. Count the remaining frogs together. Add verses whereby all the frogs jump out of the pond again so that there are "0" frogs in or out of the pond. Sing the rhyme with more or less frogs. Model the appropriate mathematical vocabulary as you support children's play, for example more, less or zero.

Foster a love for nature

Take children to a safe pond, for example at a natural habitat centre, where they can do some pond dipping and observe the creatures that live in the pond.

Create an investigative climate in your indoor and outdoor areas. Show enthusiasm when children find a worm, for example. Pose questions or "I wonder..." phrases to develop a sense of awe and stimulate inquiry. For example: "I wonder where the worm lives!" "I wonder where the worm is going!"

STORY: THE FLYING TURTLE – A STORY FROM INDIA

Once, a long long time ago, there was a village in India, and in the middle of the village, there was a large pond. Fishes swam in the pond, and the children in the village swam there. And someone else was living in that pond. A big green turtle. Every morning, he woke up and looked around him. "What a lovely morning," he said, and he sang his little song: "The sun is shining, the sky is blue and all the birds are singing." Big green turtle swam across the pond, up and down, up and down. He was waiting for his friends Mr. and Mrs. Stork to arrive. Every morning, they came to drink water from the pond and said hello to their friend the big green turtle.

"Good morning, Mr. and Mrs. Stork," said big green turtle. "And good morning to you," said the storks. "What a lovely morning," they said. "The sun is shining, the sky is blue and all the birds are singing." When they'd had a drink, Mr. and Mrs. Stork flew away. "See you tomorrow!" they called. Big green turtle waved them goodbye.

But one morning, Mr. and Mrs. Stork didn't arrive at the pond. Big green turtle looked up to see if he could see them flying overhead, but they weren't there. Instead, he saw something else. "Oh my goodness, what's that?" he said. It looked as though there was a big black cloud in the sky, but it wasn't a cloud. What big green turtle could see was the sky filled with birds, all flying away. What was happening? And then, he suddenly noticed that his feet were touching the mud at the bottom of the pond. What was happening?

Just then Mr. and Mrs. Stork flew down. They looked very worried. "What's happening?" asked big green turtle. "Why are all the birds flying away? Are you going too?" "This is what we've come to tell you," said Mr. Stork. There's no rain. The pond's drying up. The fishes are dying. And you'll die too if you stay here."

"What shall I do?" said big green turtle. "I can't fly away." "We've thought about that," said Mrs. Stork, "you haven't got wings but you've got a very strong mouth." Then, she went over to a tree and broke off a large branch. "We're going to hold this branch in our beaks, one at either end, and we want you to hold tight in the middle. Do you think you can do that?" "Yes, I think so," said big green turtle. "There's only one thing to remember," said Mr. Stork. "You mustn't open your mouth and talk to us when we're flying, because if you do you'll lose your grip and you'll fall to the ground." Big green turtle shuddered at the thought of it. "I promise not to talk," he said.

And so, they set off. Big green turtle held tight to the middle of the stick. The storks flew on and on, over fields, over hills, over villages and over the jungle. But when they flew over the jungle, one monkey looked up and said to his friend, "What's that strange thing up in the sky?" They both looked up and they couldn't help laughing when they saw big green turtle holding on to the stick. "Ha! Ha!" they laughed. "It's a flying turtle!"

Big green turtle heard them. "Don't laugh at me!" he shouted. But as soon as he opened his mouth, he lost his grip on the stick and he fell to earth. He fell … and he fell … head over heels and heels over head.

Then – SPLASH! Big green turtle fell into the river, wrong side up, just by the side of the monkeys. "Help!" he said. The monkeys swam out to him and turned him over. Turtle was crying now. "We're sorry we laughed at you," they said, "but it was a funny sight. As it happens, you're a very lucky turtle. This river is lovely. Lots of turtles live here, and there are no crocodiles!"

Big green turtle looked around. It really was very nice. "What a lovely morning," he said. "The sun's shining, the sky is blue and all the birds are singing."

Just then, Mr. and Mrs. Stork flew down. "Why didn't you do what we asked?" they said. "You could have been killed." Big green turtle hung his head. "I'm very sorry," he said. "You were very kind to take me with you and I was stupid."

"Well, let this be a lesson to you," they said. "When someone laughs at you or calls you names, don't shout back to them. Think what might happen."

"I will," said big green turtle. Mr. and Mrs. Stork flew off and big green turtle swam in the river, up and down, up and down, and looked forward to making some new friends. And every day, he sang his little song: "The sun is shining, the sky is blue and all the birds are singing."

Ways of telling

Show pictures of turtles and talk about where they live and what they eat. Ask the children whether they have seen a turtle on television or in a zoo. What did it look like? If appropriate, talk about turtles being endangered, and get some information from the Internet.

Use actions

Use your eyes to look up to see the sun shining and cup your ears to hear the birds sing. Use your arms to show the storks flying down to the pond and dip your head as you mimic the storks drinking. Point to the ceiling as you mimic the monkeys looking up and laughing at the flying turtle.

Chant or sing

Make up a simple repetitive la-la tune for turtle's song – "The sun is shining, the sky is blue and all the birds are singing" – and encourage the children to join in. Share your enjoyment of the story as you chant the repeating tunes and words with the children.

Vary the tone of your voice

Use a slow, stern voice when you tell the turtle off and a sad, sorry voice when the turtle realises he has been very silly. Use your eyes for effect. Make cross or sorry faces as you tell the story.

Early literacy

Left to right sequencing

Use objects or picture cards to sequence the story. Encourage children to suggest different outcomes. What would happen if the turtle is carried away before the drought? What if the turtle had not opened his mouth while he was being carried? How would that story end?

Phonological awareness

Write the word turtle. Explore the -urt sound in "turtle" and invite children to think of other words that have the same "u" sound, such as hurt, spurt and blurt. Introduce different spellings for the same sound, such as turtle with a "u" and shirt with an "i".

Set up resources for children to play with words. For example, provide a magnetic board with magnetic letters, white boards with dry-wipe markers, a selection of old newspapers and mazazines with with scissors and glue, "Scrabble" letters, letter cards or letter dice.

Introduce non-fiction publications

Encourage children to find out more about the lives of endangered animals. Provide a range of non-fiction books and allow children to explore a safe website.

Playful maths

Provide different weighing devices, if possible, including a hanging scale. Remind children of the story and the bundle the storks carried in their beaks. Encourage children to talk about weights. Challenge them to compare different bundles and express how heavy or light they feel. Build children's mathematical fluency by modelling vocabulary such as heavy/light, heavier than, lighter than.

Re-present the story

Invite the children to draw, paint or model their favourite part of the story. Discuss children's creations with them. Display these in a story area with names and captions of what children say.

Role play

Provide small world items to represent different parts of the story. Join in with children's play and encourage them to develop different solutions to the problem of drought.

Links to published books

The Story of the Dancing Frog by Quentin Blake

This is the story of the friendship between Great Aunt Gertrude Godkin and George the Dancing Frog, who danced so beautifully that he became famous all over the world and saved Gertrude's life. Exquisitely illustrated by the author.

Think of an Eel by Karen Wallace

Part of the Read and Wonder series, this beautifully illustrated book tells the life story of the eel and is packed with fascinating facts. It draws readers in with the first poetic sentence: "There's a warm, weedy sea to the south of Bermuda. It's called the Sargasso…."

Over and under the pond by Kate Messner, illustrated by Christopher Silas Neal

First published in 2017. This beautifully illustrated book of pond scenes is presented as experienced by a mother and son on a boat ride. The book is full of animals, plants and sounds, over and under the pond. The language is rich with descriptions, for example of wiggly quicksilver minnows.

Take time on each page, and invite children to spot other creatures and sights in the pictures, not mentioned in the text. The story follows a repetitive structure to encourage participation and early reading. Use the book to help children appreciate all the creatures and plants that thrive in ponds, and understand the need to protect such environments.

9 Cats and kittens

DOI: 10.4324/9781003358633-14

Rhymes and stories in this chapter

- Rhyme 1: The three little kittens
- Rhyme 2 for the very young: One, two, three, four
- Story: Mr. Cat and Miss Mouse

Overarching themes

- Care for animals and other living things
- Celebrating diversity
- Friendship

Glossary

grain – the seeds of wheat or corn
hay – dried grass for animals to feed on in the winter
mittens – gloves with two compartments: four fingers in one section and the thumb
 in the other

RHYMES

Introduce the main theme

Cats and kittens feature in lots of stories and rhymes for young children. The children you teach will probably be able to tell you some of these as well as having their own stories to tell about their own pet cats. Ask questions like:

- What does your cat like to eat?
- What's the naughtiest thing your cat has done?
- Where does your cat sleep?

Rhyme 1

The three little kittens
The three little kittens,

They lost their mittens,
And they began to cry:
Oh Mother, dear,
See here, see here,
Our mittens we have lost!

What? Lost your mittens?
You naughty kittens!
Now you shall have no pie.
Miaow, miaow,
We shall have no pie.

The three little kittens,
They found their mittens,
And they began to cry:
Oh Mother, dear,
See here, see here,
Our mittens we have found!

What? Found your mittens?
You good little kittens!
Now you shall have some pie.
Miaow, miaow,
We shall have some pie!

Enjoy the rhyme together

Invite the children to tell you about a cat they know or their own cat. Make a cat area in the room with a sleeping basket, a pet carrier, some cat toys and other items.

Ask the children to tell you about a time when they lost an item of clothing. What did their parents or carers say? Would they be as cross as the kittens' mother? How do their parents try to stop their children losing their gloves or mittens?

Read or chant the poem with lots of expression in your voice to reflect the frightened kittens who are admitting that they've lost their mittens, the response of their angry mother, then the relief as the kittens find their mittens and look forward to having their pie for supper.

The poem does not tell us where the kittens found their mittens, so ask the children for their own ideas about this.

You could introduce the children to Beatrix Potter's The Tale of Tom Kitten because this story has a similar theme. (Please see Links with published books at the end of this chapter.)

Early literacy

Introduce non-fiction publications

Collect information books about cats and kittens and make a display of these, reading them aloud to the children and inviting them to borrow them. Help children to use the table of contents to find particular information.

Talk about how to look after cats and kittens. Read about this and use the Internet to help you. Books for children on cat management can be found at the end of this chapter.

Read story books about cats

Encourage children to choose their favourite cat stories from the display of books. If possible, have a soft cat or make simple stick puppets to bring the stories to life.

(See the end of this chapter for a selection of these books.)

Phonological awareness

Draw attention to the rhyming pattern of *cry* and *pie*, and *kittens* and *mittens*. Put the words on a whiteboard, pointing out the pattern and the different initial sounds, and say the two words aloud with the children. Invite children to suggest more known or made up words to rhyme with these.

Writing

Introduce a lost and found noticeboard in your room and invite children and their parents to post their lost and found messages. Talk about the kind of information that is needed on each notice to help people to look out for it, for example the kind of object that's lost, the colour, size, how long it has been missing and where it was last seen.

Encourage creativity

Invite the children to draw, paint or photograph their own cat and then write the cat's name under the picture, together with some information about the cat. Display these pictures with the books about cats, or make a book to share with everyone.

Invite each child to make their own mask from card, illustrating it to represent a cat's face. Thread elastic so the masks fit round the children's ears or their head. The children can use their masks to perform their own version of the poem.

Ideas to inspire very young children

Rhyme 3

> *One, two, three, four*
> One, two, three, four,
> Four little pussy cats came to my door.
> They just stood there and said "Good-day",
> Then they tiptoed right away.

Enjoy the rhyme together

Chant the rhyme together, emphasising the rhythm and the repetition and invite the children to join in. This is a counting rhyme, so use your fingers to represent the cats, or use finger puppets, removing them one at a time or keeping your finger tucked behind the others. Pause to count how many cats are left.

Playful maths

Make a collection of other counting rhymes and invite the children to join in with these. Well-known counting rhymes include the following: *One, two, three, four, five, Once I caught a fish alive; One man went to mow; Ten green bottles; Five current buns in a baker's shop; One, two, buckle my shoe.* (The full text of these, and suggestions for other rhymes, can be found on the Internet.) Invent your own counting rhymes using favourite objects and familiar names.

Foster a love of nature

Consider ways of allowing children to care for animals in your setting and enjoy their company. If it is not possible to keep an animal in your setting, then you might consider arranging for families to bring in their pets safely to show children and talk to them about how they care for them.

There are a number of important issues to consider before including an animal as part of the nursery environment. Thorough risk and cost analyses are therefore needed before you decide to take on full responsibility for a pet.

Take young children to a working farm, if possible, so they can observe the animals and talk about them.

STORY: MR. CAT AND MISS MOUSE

Once upon a time, Mr. Cat and Miss Mouse were having fun chasing each other around the house:

Mr. Cat and Miss Mouse
Played in the house....

But Mr. Cat was so rough that he bit Miss Mouse's tail off. "Ouch," said Miss Mouse, "give me my tail back." "Not just yet," said Mr. Cat. "I'll give you your tail back when you go and see Mrs. Cow and get me some milk."

So Miss Mouse ran out and waved good-bye,
Then she saw Mrs. Cow, and she said, "Oh, my"....

"Please, Mrs. Cow, will you give me some milk, then I can give the milk to Mr. Cat, and then Mr. Cat will give me my tail back." "Not just yet," said Mrs. Cow, "you can have some milk when you go and see Mrs. Farmer and get me some hay."

So Miss Mouse ran out and waved good-bye,
Then she saw Mrs. Farmer, and she said, "Oh, my"....

"Please, Mrs. Farmer, will you give me some hay, then I can give the hay to Mrs. Cow and she will give me some milk, then I can give the milk to Mr. Cat, and then he will give me my tail back." "Not just yet," said Mrs. Farmer, "you can have some hay when you go and see Mr. Butcher and get me some meat."

So Miss Mouse ran out and waved good-bye,
Then she saw Mr. Butcher, and she said, "Oh, my"....

"Please, Mr. Butcher, will you give me some meat, then I can give the meat to Mrs. Farmer, then she will give me some hay, then I can give the hay to Mrs. Cow, and then she will give me some milk, then I can give the milk to Mr. Cat, and then he will give me my tail back." "Not just yet," said Mr. Butcher, "you can have some meat when you go and see Miss Baker and get me some bread."

So Miss Mouse ran out and waved good-bye,
Then she saw Miss Baker, and she said, "Oh, my"....

"Please, Miss Baker, will you give me some bread, so I can give the bread to Mr. Butcher, then he will give me some meat, then I can give the meat to Mrs. Farmer, then she will give me some hay, then I can give the hay to Mrs. Cow, and then she will give me some milk, then I can give the milk to Mr. Cat, and then he will give me my tail back." "Yes," said Miss Baker, "you can have some bread as long as you promise you'll never eat my grain again." "I promise," said Miss Mouse. And so....

Miss Baker gave Miss Mouse some bread and Miss Mouse gave the bread to Mr. Butcher.

Mr. Butcher gave Miss Mouse some meat and Miss Mouse gave the meat to Mrs. Farmer.

Mrs. Farmer gave Miss Mouse some hay and Miss Mouse gave the hay to Mrs. Cow.

Mrs. Cow gave Miss Mouse some milk and Miss Mouse gave the milk to Mr. Cat.

Mr. Cat gave Miss Mouse her tail back and everyone was happy.

Enjoy the story together

The story-rhyme has all the features that make it exactly right for very young children to listen to and join in with, so share it with them over and over again until they are familiar with the characters and can chant the story-rhyme with you.

Ways of telling

Emphasise the rhyme, rhythm and repetition and use your eyes, facial expression and other gestures to keep the children's attention. When the children know the sequence fairly well, pause before you introduce each new character or object to encourage the children to guess who or what comes next.

Help the children to re-tell the story and remember the sequence by making puppets or cut-outs of Miss Mouse, Mr. Cat, Mrs. Cow, Mrs. Farmer, Mr. Butcher, Miss Baker and the objects mentioned in the story – Miss Mouse's tail, the milk, the hay, the meat, the bread and the grain. Invite the children to hold these up as you tell the story. The visual objects will be particularly helpful for children who are learning English as an additional language.

Make up a simple musical rhythmic chant for each repetitive part of the story, stressing the rhythm as shown here (in bold):

*So Miss **Mouse** ran **out** and **waved** good-**bye**,*
*Then she **saw** Mrs. **Cow**, and she **said**, "Oh, **my**"....*

Re-present the story

Invite children to make models of cats using modelling clay. Suggest they illustrate their favourite part of the story. Display these models and illustrations with names and captions to show the sequence of the story.

Early literacy

Accumulative stories

Make a collection of stories where each event builds on the next until a satisfying ending is reached. Here are some examples:

This is the house that Jack built....

The farmer's in his den....

There was a crooked man....

Prepare cards of each animal and character in the story, or collect small world animals and people. Invite children to sequence the story.

Use role play

Tell the story to the children and invite different children to play the part of Miss Mouse, Mr. Cat, Mrs. Cow, Mrs. Farmer, Mr. Butcher and Miss Baker so that they use their own dialogue. Use the puppets or cut-out visuals to guide the children in their re-telling.

Place the small world animals and people in the sand tray and encourage children to play out the story in their own way. Join in sensitively to layer on new vocabulary and encourage talk.

Playful maths

Help children to order the different layers of the story using ordinal numbers. First Miss Mouse went to Mrs. Cow, second to Mrs. Farmer, third to Mr. Butcher and fourth to Mr. Baker. Use ordinal numbers at different times of the day as part of children's play or embedded in routines. Invite children to spot the first, second and third daffodils to flower? Who is standing first, second, third in the line for lunch today?

Links to published books

Mog the Forgetful Cat by Judith Kerr

First published in 1970, *Mog the Forgetful Cat* has been a favourite story ever since it first appeared. It is the story of a forgetful cat who lives with the Thomas family. Different members of the family are annoyed by Mog on a daily basis, but they love her very much. One night, after many mishaps, Mog goes outside, feeling sorry for herself. She notices a burglar and frightens him in action. From being an annoying cat, she becomes a heroine and is rewarded with a medal and a special meal.

The Tale of Tom Kitten by Beatrix Potter

Mrs. Tabitha Twitchit washes and dresses her three kittens, Mittens, Tom and Moppet, in their best clothes because she is expecting friends to tea, but the kittens go out to play and lose their frocks, trousers, jacket and hat. Mrs. Twitchit is very angry and sends the kittens to their room. (You might want to use your discretion in introducing this book since Mrs Twitchit smacks her kittens before she sends them to their room. If you do wish to use it, you could tell the children that the story is over 100 years old and was written at a time when parents regularly smacked their children.)

Other well-known published books about cats include:

The Cat in the Hat by Dr. Seuss

Me and My Cat by Satoshi Kitamora

Grumpy Cat by Britta Teckentrup

Six Dinner Sid by Inga Moore

Meg and Mog series of books by Helen Nichol and Jan Pienkowski

Books about cat management

The Happy Cat Handbook by Pippa Mattinson and Lucy Easton

Cats: 101 Amazing Facts about Cats: Cat Books for Kids: Volume 1 by Jenny Kellett

10 Lots of billy goats

DOI: 10.4324/9781003358633-15

Rhymes and stories in this chapter

- Rhyme 1: Five little billy goats played by the shore
- Rhyme 2 for the very young: I'm a little billy goat
- Story: Three Billy Goats Gruff

Overarching themes

- Working together as a group to find solutions to problems and improve communities
- Helping each other to overcome difficulties

Glossary

billy goat – a male goat
butt – to hit something or someone with the head or horns
clamber – to walk or climb through rough ground
kid – a young goat
nanny goat – a female goat

RHYMES

Introduce the main theme

Some of the children might know the story of The Three Billy Goats Gruff or The Wolf and the Seven Little Kids. If so, they will be able to tell you what happens in these stories. Rural children or children who have visited a city farm might also have tales to tell you about goats. However, it is also possible that some children might never have seen a goat, so have some pictures and photos ready to show them and encourage them to talk about the characteristic features of goats (the shape of their eyes, their horns, their ears, their colouring, their size and the language to describe them – billy goats, nanny goats and kids and so on).

Rhyme 1:

Five little billy goats played by the shore
Five little billy goats played by the shore,

One swam out to sea, and then there were four.
Four little billy goats climbed up a tree,
One fell down, and then there were three.
Three little billy goats heard a cow go *Moo*,
One went to play with it, and then there were two.
Two little billy goats played in the sun,
One went to fly a kite, and then there was one.
One little billy goat cried all afternoon,
So they put him in a rocket, and sent him to the moon.

Enjoy the rhyme together

Chant the rhyme with the children over and over again until they are familiar with the words. If you can learn the rhyme by heart, you can keep eye contact with the children and respond to their facial expressions and actions. Encourage them to join in with you. Use your fingers or invite the children to stand up to represent the billy goats, reducing the number after each couplet.

Early literacy

Stimulate talk

Ask questions about the billy goats and match these with the children's own experiences.

■ Which billy goat would you like to be? Why?

■ Have you ever flown a kite?

■ Have you swum in the sea?

■ Why was the last billy goat sad?

■ Would you like to fly to the moon?

Discuss the vocabulary

Talk about *billy goats* and explain that these are *male* goats. With very young children, you might want to say "daddy goats." Explain that *female* goats (or mummy goats) are called *nanny goats* and baby goats are called *kids*.

Phonological awareness

Draw attention to the phonic sounds and patterns. Ask the children to think of words or made-up words that rhyme with *goat*. Show them how the word is spelled, pointing out the vowel digraph *oa* and the final consonant *t*. Display other words with the same spelling pattern, like *boat*, *coat*, *moat* and *throat*.

Point to the vowel digraph *ee* in *tree* and *three* and think of other words that contain this same pattern (e.g. *bee*, *knee* and *see*).

Encourage creativity

Invite the children to design, make and decorate a kite, using a variety of skills. There are lots of ideas for kite design on the Internet. Involve the children in drawing up a plan for their kite, measuring the dimensions, cutting it out, decorating it, attaching a string and so on. Finally, on a windy day, fly your kites outside.

Playful maths

Counting

Five Little Billy Goats is a counting rhyme (see also the counting rhyme in Trees and Acorns). Use the numbers – five, four, three, two and one to help young children learn to count. Invite five children to play the parts of each billy goat, miming the actions of sitting or kneeling down as each one goes away, leaving the others standing. Pause the rhyme to count how many billy goats have gone away and how many are still standing up. Explain that the story they are going to hear later has *three* billy goats.

Ideas to inspire very young children

Rhyme 2

> ***I'm a little billy goat***
> I'm a little billy goat
> Sitting by a tree
> I get up in the morning
> And what do I see?

I'm a little billy goat
Eating fresh green hay
"Come on," says my mummy,
"It's the middle of the day."

I'm a little billy goat,
Playing with a bee,
"Come in now," says daddy,
"It's nearly time for tea."

I'm a little billy goat
Time to say goodnight
Daddy tucks me up in bed
Eyes shut tight.

Enjoy the rhyme together

Chant "I'm a little billy goat" over and over again, encouraging the children to join in if they can. Emphasise the rhythm of this rhyme. Mark the beat by clapping or using a tambour, 1, 2, for each line of the verse.

Put stress on individual words to create a "sing-song" effect. This intonation will help the children to absorb the rhythms and respond to them (e.g. *I'm* a little *bi*-lly goat *Sit*-ting by a *tree; Five* little *bi*-lly goats *played* by the *shore).*

Talk about the little billy goat and encourage the children to explore the things he did and match them to their own experiences. These questions might help.

- What do you do when you get up in the morning?

- What do you think little billy goat saw when he got up?

- What do you think his mummy wanted him to do in the middle of the day?

- What sort of game did he play with the bee?

- What do you think he had for tea?

- Why was he tired at night?

- Who put little billy goat to bed at night? Who puts you to bed at night?

Telling the time

Use the rhyme to help children talk about time. When you chant *I'm a little billy goat,* pause at the end of each verse and ask the children what time they think it is when billy goat gets up, when it is "the middle of the day", when it is "nearly time for tea" and finally when it is "time to say goodnight". Show the times on a clock-face to help the children learn about the passing of time.

Make up your own rhymes

Make up your own rhymes in response to children's interests. This will encourage children to be creative and be inventive with their own language as part of their play. Repeat children's own chants and rhymes when you join in children's self-initiated play. This will open up opportunities for them to expand their rhymes and to absorb the characteristic rhythms of rhymes for the very young.

STORY: THREE BILLY GOATS GRUFF

Once upon a time, there were Three Billy Goats. They were great friends. The first one was called Little Billy Goat Gruff, and he was the smallest; the second one was called Middle-Sized Billy Goat Gruff, and he was a little bit bigger than Little Billy Goat Gruff. The third one was called Great Big Billy Goat Gruff, and he was the biggest of all.

But even though they were of different sizes, they all *loved* the same thing – lush green grass. One day, Little Billy Goat Gruff said, "We've eaten all the grass in this field. Shall we cross the bridge and go into the next field. The grass there is lush and green and there's plenty of it for all three of us."

"There's just one problem," said Great Big Billy Goat Gruff, who knew the fields better than his friends. "A bad-tempered Troll lives under the bridge, and he doesn't like anyone crossing over it to get to the next field."

"I'm not frightened of a Troll," said Little Billy Goat Gruff. "I'll go first." And this is what he did. But as he stepped on to the bridge, he heard a loud voice calling:

"Who's that trip-trapping over my bridge?"

Little Billy Goat Gruff was brave. "It's me. Little Billy Goat Gruff," he shouted back. "I just want to eat the grass on the other side of the bridge."

"Well, I'm going to come and eat you up!" said the Troll.

Little Billy Goat Gruff thought quickly. "Don't do that," he said, "I'm very small. Wait till Middle-Sized Billy Goat Gruff comes over the bridge. He's much bigger than me, and he'll make you a better meal." And so, the Troll let Little Billy Goat Gruff cross the bridge and he began to eat the lush green grass on the other side.

"My turn now," said Middle-Sized Billy Goat Gruff. But as he stepped on to the bridge, he heard a loud voice calling:

"Who's that trip-trapping over my bridge?"

Middle-Sized Billy Goat Gruff was brave. "It's me. Middle-Sized Billy Goat Gruff," he shouted back. "I just want to eat the grass on the other side of the bridge."

"Well, I'm going to eat you up!" said the Troll.

Middle-Sized Billy Goat Gruff thought quickly. "Don't do that," he said, "I'm only middle-sized. Wait till Great Big Billy Goat Gruff comes over the bridge. He's much bigger than me, and he'll make you a better meal." And so, the Troll let Middle-Sized Billy Goat Gruff cross the bridge and he began to eat the lush green grass on the other side.

"My turn now," said Great Big Billy Goat Gruff. But as he stepped on to the bridge, he heard a loud voice calling:

"Who's that trip-trapping over my bridge?"

Great Big Billy Goat Gruff was brave. "It's me. Great Big Billy Goat Gruff," he shouted back. "I just want to eat the lush green grass on the other side of the bridge."

"Well, I'm going to eat you up!" said the Troll.

Great Big Billy Goat Gruff thought quickly. "Come up on the bridge so I can see you," he said. And so, the Troll clambered up on to the bridge. Without more ado, Great Big Billy Goat Gruff lowered his head and butted the Troll with his powerful horns. The Troll fell into the river.

And so, Great Big Billy Goat Gruff joined his two friends on the other side of the bridge and they all enjoyed eating the lush green grass. What's more, the Troll was never seen again.

Ways of telling

Encourage the children to join in with the repeated phrases: *Who's that trip-trapping over my bridge?* and *Well, I'm going to eat you up.*

Use lots of expression and a range of voices for the three goats and the Troll, letting your voice tones get deeper and louder for the larger goats and for the Troll. Use your eyes and face to show the goats' sense of fear, excitement and bravery. These gestures will help the children when they enact their own role play based on the story.

Early literacy

Discuss the vocabulary

Encourage the children to ask about words they might not have met before. For example, they will probably not have met the word *lush*. Can they guess what kind of grass Little Billy Goat Gruff was looking at? Explain that the grass is very green, thick and soft. You might also want to explain the definition of the verbs *clambered* and *butted*.

Talk about adjectives that denote difference

Adjectives that denote difference are called *superlative* adjectives, but there is no need to use this term if the children are not ready to learn it. Some examples are as follows: *big, bigger* and *biggest*; *small, smaller* and *smallest*; *tall, taller* and *tallest*; *hot, hotter* and *hottest*. Ask the children to think of more examples and write these up for them to see. Point out the pattern of endings: *er* and *est*.

Foster a love of nature

Grow some grass seeds in a tray. Encourage the children to feel the seeds and talk about them. Water the tray every day and observe the grass as it grows. Ask the children to measure the growth and talk about what the shoots look like and how green they are. Use the word *lush* to describe your grass to help the children understand what this term means.

Playful maths

Learn about ordinal numbers

Following on from the counting rhyme above, help the children to learn about *first, second* and *third*, using the story as a prompt. Refer back to the five billy goats in the counting rhyme and introduce the ordinals *fourth* and *fifth*.

Play games with the children to encourage an understanding of ordinal numbers. For example, you could pose challenges, for example if you're the third person in the line, please sit down. If you're the fourth child in the line, please tap your head. Display a calendar and name the date every day with the children, for example today is the fifth day of February.

Use mathematical vocabulary

Collect sets of familiar objects of different sizes, for example cereal packets, teddy bears and wellington boots. Use mathematical vocabulary to compare

■ lengths and heights, for example long/short, longer/shorter or tall/short

■ mass and weight, for example heavy/light, heavier than or lighter than

Role play

Set up an outdoor billy goats gruff area to encourage role play. Suggest that the children take on the parts of the goats and the Troll. Encourage them to use different voices for the characters and to use expression – your own re-telling will help the children enormously because they can learn from your use of voice and expression. Encourage the children to perform their version of the story to the rest of the group or to family members.

Re-present the story

Encourage the children to draw or paint their favourite part of the story. Talk about each child's contribution and display their creations on the wall. Older children might be able to write captions to enhance their drawing or painting.

Link to a published book

We're going on a bear hunt by Michael Rosen and Helen Oxenbury

First published in 1989, this is a very popular book with both teachers and young children. A family go out looking for a bear, not expecting to find one. They encounter obstacles and challenges on their way, including a snow storm, a deep river, a forest and long, wavy grass. It is an excellent book for exploring sounds, like "Swishy swashy, swishy swashy, swishy swashy" grass. Each time they face a challenge, they chant together: "Oh no! We can't go over it. We can't go under it. We'll have to go through it!" They face their difficulties as a team and help each other across the different terrains. Like the Three Billy Goats, they encounter a dreaded creature, a real bear, at the end of their search. Unlike the billy goats, they run back home and hide back under the bed covers. I wonder what happened to the Troll or the bear?

Michael Rosen performs the story with great expression on this YouTube video. Helen Oxenbury's pictures form the backdrop. https://youtu.be/2OI7fe766nk?si=jy7 484IpBDkImb5s

Afterword

Our central aim in writing this book has been to encourage you to become the teller of rhymes and stories and to share your favourite ones spontaneously with the children you work with. The book is both practical and theoretical. We wanted not only to offer some ideas to get you started but also to give you a rationale for adopting this approach so that you feel sure of the value of live rhymes and stories for young children's learning and development.

We wanted the practical chapters to support your work with young children. Our aim has been for you to enjoy making the connection between yourself and your young listeners as you hold their attention with your eyes, use your voice and your gestures to add drama and sparkle to your words and then monitor their reactions as they create their own individual and shared responses.

The three theoretical chapters in this book will hopefully have persuaded you that oral rhyming and storying must surely form an integral part of the early years and primary curricula, in part because they help to develop children's interest in language use. But crucially, we have argued that stories and rhymes enter children's consciousness by enhancing their knowledge of the world and helping them to develop imaginative and emotional insights into their own lives and the lives of other people. This is the unequalled power of rhymes and stories.

We hope that you will use the practical chapters to help you get started and the theoretical chapters to underpin your work. It is important that you then reflect on your experiences of sharing rhymes and stories. This is in order to inform your teaching and help you develop your own unique approach in response to the needs and interests of the children you work with. This work is done in relationship with the children and in partnership with the families and communities in your circle. We hope that families will share their rhymes and stories from different parts of the world to build a rich and diverse repertoire, help children feel valued and expand their knowledge and understanding of the world.

DOI: 10.4324/9781003358633-16

For those of you who have not yet told a story or recited a rhyme without a book in your hand, we hope we have given you the confidence to be adventurous and to put this book aside as you share in the pleasure of creating a world of the imagination for children. Every rhyme and story is a magical world in itself, so please have a go at fashioning each one into your own unique work of art so that it feels joyous, colourful, exciting and surprising for both you and your young listeners.

Sarah Cousins and Hilary Minns

May 2023

Sources consulted

Many of the stories we have included here will be familiar to readers. In order to be as authentic as possible, we have sourced older or original sources and retold our own versions of these stories in a way that helps to make them accessible to a young audience. We have tried to use language and structural forms that will help you, the storyteller, to read the stories seamlessly or, better still, to learn the key events so that it is easier for you to share the stories in your own words without using the book.

The Elves and the Shoemaker appears as The Little Elves in Grimm's Fairy Tales, published by Walter Scott Publishing in 1905. It is translated by Lucy Crane.

The Little Red Hen is an American folk tale by Mary Mapes Dodge. It first appeared in Volume 12 of St. Nicholas Magazine (September 1874).

The Enormous Turnip is based on an old Russian tale. Our retelling is adapted from The Turnip in Russian Tales for Children by Aleksei Tolstoy, published by Routledge and Sons in 1944.

The Monkeys and the Crocodile is an original story that uses structures and rhymes that will be familiar to young children but in a more exotic setting.

The two Greek fables we have retold here, *The North Wind and the Sun* and *George the Town Mouse and Henry the Country Mouse*, were originally ascribed to Aesop and date from the 6th century BCE. Across the centuries, there have been numerous revisions of these two stories and the fact that they continue to be revised and retold today attests to their importance. Our retellings are based on The Sun and the Wind and The Country Mouse and the City Mouse retold by Sara Cone Bryant in Stories to Tell to Children, published by G. Harrap (1911).

The Girl who gave her Precious Doll is based on an old folk tale from the tradition of the Comanche people who lived in present-day Texas in the 18th and 19th centuries. There are several retellings of this beautiful story. We are grateful to The British and Foreign School Society and its Director, Joanne Knight, for permission to retell our version of "A Legend for the Forget-Me-Not." This story appears in Creation Stories (London, BFSS National R.E. Centre, 1995).

The Flying Turtle is an oral story that Mrs. Mohinder Mudhar listened to as a child when she was growing up in India. She recorded her own version of the story for children to listen to in a Coventry primary school. We are grateful to Mrs. Mudhar for giving us permission to retell our version of the story here.

Mr Cat and Miss Mouse is our retelling of The Cat and the Mouse, which can be found in the 1942 edition of Joseph Jacobs' English Fairy Tales (London, Frederick Muller).

The Three Billy Goats Gruff was originally collected by Peter Christen Asbjørnsen and Jørgen Moe in their Norske Folkeeventyr, first published between 1841 and 1844. The first version in English appeared in George Webbe Dasent's Popular Tales from the Norse (1859) in which he translated of some of the Norse tales.

Sources for nursery rhymes

Many well-known nursery rhymes were written down in the 18th century or even earlier. Nobody knows who wrote them down originally, and they often appear as "Anon" in later publications. We have chosen a selection of these rhymes for two reasons; firstly, they link nicely with the overall theme of each particular chapter, and secondly, Sarah has shared them over the years with young children and knows from first-hand experience how popular they are.

The words and phrases we have used here often differ from those used in the original rhymes we have researched. Sometimes we have adapted them to foreground a particular character or theme, and at other times, we have used Sarah's version because it worked well with the children she taught.

We have written six rhymes ourselves in order to make a connection with particular stories because, even after extensive searching, we could not find a traditional rhyme that reflected key aspects of the theme that we particularly wanted to emphasise. They are *The Swampy River Crocodile* (Part II, Chapter 4); *Monkey monkey, mangrove tree* (Part II, Chapter 4); *Mrs Mouse finds a House* (Part II, Chapter 5); *What's that there?* (Part II, Chapter 8); *I'm a little billy goat* (Part II, Chapter 10), *Five little billy goats played by the shore* (Part II, Chapter 10).

Three of the rhymes, *Cock-a-doodle-doo* (Part II, Chapter 1), *Pat-a-cake, pat-a-cake* (Part II, Chapter 2) and *Hickory dickory dock* (Part II, Chapter 5) first appeared in written form in *Tom Thumb's Pretty Song Book* (1744?) They were also published in *Tommy Thumb's song book, for all little masters and misses, to be sung to them by their nurses, until they can sing themselves.* By Nurse Lovechild. Worcester, Massachusetts Cengage Gale (1788). The British Library holds a copy of both these books.

Pussy cat, pussy cat, where have you been? (Part II, Chapter 5) and *The north wind doth blow* (Part II, Chapter 6) are both taken from Songs from the Nursery, London, R. Phillips (1812), in the British Library.

Three blind mice (Part II, Chapter 5) appears as a musical round in Deuteromelia: or the seconde part of Musicks melodie (1609). The author is Thomas Ravenscroft, and the volume can be viewed in the British Library.

The three little kittens (Part II, Chapter 9) was possibly written by Eliza Lee Follen and appears in New Nursery Songs for All Good Children (1868). This volume can be viewed in the British Library.

Cobbler, cobbler, mend my shoe (Part II, Chapter 1) can be found in Unison Songs for Children, together with other songs compiled by Robert Coverley. It was published by Darewski in c. 1936 and can be viewed in the British Library. Iona and Peter Opie in the Oxford Dictionary of Nursery Rhymes (1951) write that this rhyme also appeared in Original Ditties for the Nursery (J. Harris) c. 1805.

Oats and beans and barley grow (Part II, Chapter 3) is a traditional British and American folk song. It is number 1380 in Steve Roud's Folk Song Index, in which he has collected songs from the oral tradition in English from across the world. The British Library has an audio recording of the song made between 1960 and 1967: Singing games: King William, etc.

We have included five popular counting rhymes in our selection:

One, two, three, four, Monkeys on the forest floor (Part II, Chapter 4) is adapted from the rhyme in Nursery Calculations (W. Belch) c. 1815.

It hasn't been possible to trace the origin of the other four counting rhymes:

Five little peas in a pea-pod pressed (Part II, Chapter 3)

One, two, three, four, four little pussy cats came to my door (Part II, Chapter 9)

Five little cuddly dolls (Part II, Chapter 7)

Five little speckled frogs (Part II, Chapter 8)

It has been difficult to trace the origin of the following nine rhymes, though they appear to be "Anon":

Rap-a-tap-a-rap-a-tap (Part II, Chapter 1)

I went into the baker's shop (Part II, Chapter 2)

I had a little marigold seed (Part II, Chapter 3)

Flowers grow like this (Part II, Chapter 3)

Tippy, tippy, tippy, tippy (Part II, Chapter 5)

Whether the weather be fine (Part II, Chapter 6)

I hear raindrops (Part II, Chapter 6)

Miss Polly had a dolly (Part II, Chapter 7)

Teddy bear, teddy bear, turn around (Part II, Chapter 7)

As Iona and Peter Opie (1984) prefaced in *The Oxford Nursery Rhyme Book,* "these rhymes are the happy heritage of oral tradition" (p. v). These unstoppable collectors acknowledged that, for over 200 years, many different versions of rhymes were encapsulated in print. Nevertheless, we share their belief that "oral tradition recognizes no 'correct' versions: the only defensible version is how one knows it oneself" (p. vi).

Index

For Product Safety Concerns and Information please contact our EU
representative GPSR@taylorandfrancis.com Taylor & Francis Verlag GmbH,
Kaufingerstraße 24, 80331 München, Germany

Printed and bound by CPI Group (UK) Ltd, Croydon, CR0 4YY

08/06/2025

01897000-0019